ADHD RAISING AN EXPLOSIVE CHILD

Everything You Need to Know About ADHD Is Found Here, a Complete Guide of Advantages, Methods, Treatments, Medication and More to Help You with Your Explosive Child

D1528618

Table of Contents

Introduction

The term "explosive" is a very strong word with loaded connotations. It implies a person who is violent, unpredictable, and dangerous. So, the term "explosive child" understandably evokes fear in parents. But explosive children are not always synonymous with abusive children or disruptive children. In fact, many parents find their child explosively angry for extended periods of time but do not think of this type of anger as necessarily harmful to self or others (or as what most people would call "malicious"). The fact that some youngsters with extraordinarily explosive wrath act out less in situations where they can damage others and behave more normally in situations where they cannot support this theory. The disruptive behavior of an explosive child is usually not as extreme as that of a child with an oppositional defiant disorder (ODD).

Unlike the anger of a child with ODD, which is not necessarily a problem but is often thought to be "misunderstood," the anger of an explosive child may be premeditated and purposeful. It may also make him seem to have antisocial tendencies. Explosive children can be disruptive, harmful, and even violent. They may engage in such behaviors as hitting, biting, kicking, and screaming to get their own way. An explosive child can also destroy property or hurt himself by hitting his head on the wall. Such actions are intended to get the attention of adults or peers and/or to evoke a reaction as a way of getting what he wants.

Parents of explosive children often attempt to teach their child not to hit and kick by telling him not to do it and by giving him timeouts or other forms of discipline if he does it anyway. However, these techniques rarely work with an explosive child because of his relatively low level of frustration tolerance (see below). He often goes on to do more intense behaviors that are intended to cause more immediate discomfort.

The term "explosive anger" is a misnomer because the anger of an explosive child is not always explosive. In fact, people with ADHD (attention deficit hyperactivity disorder) are often seen as more likely to display explosive behavior than their counterparts without ADHD. This has resulted in research in which researchers have tried to identify characteristics of "explosive children" in order to make mental health professionals better able to diagnose and treat them (for example, see Lynam and Facer, 1991).

Because children with ADHD are often more obvious in the classroom and can be more disruptive than other children, they are more likely to be identified as having mental health problems. By contrast, students without ADHD who display similar behavior may not be identified as having such problems and may only receive inattentive diagnoses (such as ADD or a less severe version of ODD). This is especially true if they are otherwise academically gifted and/or high achievers. Thus, they may not receive the same level of support or intervention that an ADHD child receives at school. Also, parents of these children may not identify their child's attentional difficulties as being a problem because he is so high achieving.

Chapter 1. Understanding What ADHD Is

ADHD is a mental health disorder that causes a mix of hyperactivity and impulsive behaviors. Children are frequently "targeted" by this disorder, but adults are known to suffer from it as well.

ADHD is extremely common to the point that some even dub it to be one of the single most widespread neurodevelopmental disorders of childhood. It's estimated that more than 6.1 million children in the U.S. have been diagnosed with ADHD so far (according to studies released in 2016) (CDC, 2021).

The symptoms can range from mild to severe depending on how many aspects of a person are affected by this disorder. Most times, symptoms tend to vary over time, and adults suffering from ADHD tend to have milder symptoms than they did in childhood. However, adults are suffering from severe ADHD symptoms as well which can impair their daily lives.

Adults suffering from ADHD usually have trouble staying focused at work, in school, and even in their personal lives. They're also more prone than the overall population to be unemployed or underemployed, to have marital problems, to divorce at a higher rate, and to suffer from a variety of mental health issues.

This is precisely why tackling ADHD in childhood is extremely important—it's not just about your peace of mind as a parent but also about the future of your child.

What Does It Mean to Have ADHD?

Living with ADHD can be tough both for the parents and for the children. The good news is that it's possible to live very happily even with ADHD. As you will see in this book, there are plenty of things you can do as a parent to help your child grow healthier, stay more focused, and, generally, be better, both during childhood and as future adults.

So, what does it mean to have ADHD?

Let's tackle what it doesn't mean. ADHD is not just a medical name for a child with a bit more energy than usual. All children have plenty of energy and that's a sign they are healthy, both mentally and physically.

However, when the energy is misplaced, too much, and it prevents the child from learning, growing up, and living a life similar to that of other children his/her age, it can become a problem.

In short, having ADHD means the child has trouble paying attention, completing tasks, and following instructions when compared to peers of the same age. It can also mean the child is easily distracted by his/her own thoughts or other people around him/her; doesn't follow through on plans to do a certain activity because he/she loses interest quickly, and may have difficulty organizing tasks in an orderly manner.

Types of ADHD

Like many other mental health disorders, ADHD comes in different variations:

- **Predominantly inattentive type:** People with this version of the disorder are often forgetful, have difficulty focusing on tasks at hand, and may not realize when they need to turn in work. They also tend to lose things easily, misplace items frequently, or be sloppy about their appearance. These symptoms can make them seem lazy or disorganized.
- **Predominantly hyperactive-impulsive type:** This is typically the most severe form of ADHD. People with this condition have a hard time sitting still and may be excessively talkative, fidgety, or impulsive. They are often restless during the day and interrupt others without realizing what they're doing (even if it's making other people mad).
- **Combined type:** Those diagnosed with this specific type of ADHD have both symptoms of inattentiveness and hyperactivity/impulsivity.

Comprehending ADHD

One of the sad truths about ADHD is that, like other mental health disorders (depression, anxiety, and so on), it is not fully understood. We do understand quite a lot about it at this point. Though we know enough to build treatment schemes and help both children and adults suffering from this attention disorder. At the end of the day though, the complex, intrinsic mechanisms and psychopathology of ADHD are not fully understood.

ADHD Types of Symptoms and Characteristics of a Child With ADHD

Keep in mind that no mental health disorder should ever be diagnosed at home. If you notice any of the following symptoms, you should definitely consult with a specialist for a diagnosis.

14

So, what are the symptoms and characteristics of a child with ADHD (Healthline, 2020)?

- Hyperactivity
- Impulsiveness
- Inattention/disorganization
- Excessive daydreaming or talking
- Self-focused behavior
- Interrupting
- Having trouble waiting for their turn
- Fidgeting
- Emotional turmoil
- Cannot play quietly
- Frequently doesn't finish tasks
- Avoiding mental effort of any kind

While these are not all symptoms a child with ADHD might experience, they are among the more common ones, so you should definitely keep them in mind.

ADHD Etiological Classification

In a traditional understanding of the disorder, ADHD is caused by a dopamine deficiency; it's a decreased blood flow in the prefrontal cortex and cerebellum part of the brain, as well as the ganglia, which has an important role in creating dopamine.

ADHD can be triggered by an array of causes and, as such, scientists have categorized this disorder according to its cause (which is referred to as an "etiological classification").

Here are the main categories you should be aware of here (Kessler, 2021):

- Inattentive ADHD is caused by dopamine deficiency and insufficient activity in the prefrontal cortex.
- Over focused ADHD is caused by dopamine and serotonin deficiencies, as well as overactive anterior cingulate gyrus.
- Temporal lobe ADHD is caused by too much activity in the limbic part of the brain and by decreased activity in the prefrontal cortex (regardless of whether the child is focusing on a task or at rest).
- Ring of Fire ADHD is caused by too much activity in the entire brain, including the cerebral cortex and other areas.
- Anxious ADHD is a combination of anxiety and ADD and is caused by high activity in the basal ganglia area of the brain.

Each of these types of ADHD comes with its own set of symptoms and specific treatment, but we will get into this a little later on in the book.

The ADHD Brain

While we cannot fully understand what happens in the human brain when it is affected by certain disorders (ADHD included), we do have a very good idea of how the brain reacts to these problems.

In the case of ADHD, it is believed that the brain has a problem with its dopamine production which causes it to be less able to tune out distractions.

Dopamine is very tightly linked with a neurotransmitter called norepinephrine, and when there is an issue in its production, the dopamine levels are affected as well. Since dopamine is the neurotransmitter dealing with the pleasure center of the brain, an imbalance in its levels can translate into a series of symptoms many of which can fall under the ADHD umbrella.

It is not exactly clear how ADHD develops and multiple theories have been raised.

One theory of ADHD's cause states that certain connections within the frontal lobe make an individual more susceptible to impulsive behavior, including hyperactivity or lack of focus on one task.

Other theories state that when the brain suffers from ADHD, a person has less of an inhibitory response to stimuli in the environment and is unable to filter out what it considers unimportant.

For some people with ADHD to focus or concentrate on something without being distracted by other things, they need more stimulus than others.

Some studies have found that ADHD is largely hereditary and that there might be a genetic link. Children and siblings of someone who suffers from ADHD are more likely to develop the disorder as well (NHS, 2021). Of course, this is not always the case, but research shows there is a higher likelihood in this direction.

What's the Difference Between ADD and ADHD?

When you start reading about attention deficit hyperactivity disorder, you might get confused by the fact that you will see it shortened to both ADD and ADHD. In reality, there is no difference between the two. ADHD is the unanimously accepted current version of this disorder's name. ADD is an outdated version of the same name, mostly used to describe inattentive-type ADHD (but since more discoveries have been made in this field, we now know that this is not the only type of ADHD there is).

Every child with ADHD is different—the symptoms they experience can be wildly different as well. Learning how to spot the first symptoms and when to call for the services of a medical professional are crucial steps in parenting a child with attention deficit hyperactivity disorder—precisely because they will help you better manage the situation in the future.

In this chapter, we will dig more into the topic of ADHD symptoms and how parents can spot them early (or at least as early as possible).

ADHD Symptoms at Every Age

ADHD diagnosis can sometimes be tricky because a child has to show six (or more) symptoms, from the list we will share with you below, for more than six months. Usually, the diagnosis of ADHD can be made at any time between the age of 4 and the age of 16. Keep an eye out for indicators of ADHD in your child around puberty if you feel he or she has it. The frequency of symptoms is just as important as noting when the symptoms first appeared and how the child is affected when you are seeking a diagnosis.

There are two large categories of symptoms that can help you identify ADHD in a child. The first category is related to inattention while the second one is related to hyperactivity; both are essential components of ADHD.

Inattention-related symptoms include trouble with the following:

- Paying attention to details or making careless mistakes
- Focusing on tasks or even during playtime
- Listening when an adult is speaking to them directly, even when the adult is in a position of authority (like a parent or a teacher)
- Following instructions on tasks, homework, or chores
- Organizing their tasks and activities
- Completing tasks that require them to focus or devote mental effort for longer periods

- Keeping track of their things (school supplies, phone, glasses, and so on)
- Avoiding distractions
- Remembering things when they are running a daily activity

Hyperactivity-related symptoms include having trouble with the following:

- Fidgeting, tapping their hands or their feet, squirming, and so on
- Standing up and getting away from their seat in situations where they should remain seated (such as at school or in the church)
- Running and climbing in places and situations they shouldn't be doing this
- The ability to take part in certain activities quietly
- Feeling like they are permanently on-the-going
- Talking excessively
- Answering rapidly before the question is even spelled out
- Interrupting conversations and games

Most of these symptoms are seen frequently in children and teenagers with ADHD. However, as mentioned above, one or two of these symptoms, popping up sporadically, do not necessarily lead to a diagnosis of ADHD. Furthermore, every child or teenager will behave differently and there are, of course, differences between how children and teenagers behave (e.g., teens might be more inclined towards reckless behavior).

Adult ADHD is rarely diagnosed and there's insufficient research in this area. This is mostly because, with ADHD being a developmental disorder, it is assumed that an adult with ADHD will have already been diagnosed in childhood. Generally, by the age of 25, about 15% of the adults diagnosed with ADHD as children will still have the full range of symptoms and 65% will experience symptoms that affect their daily lives (NHS, 2021).

In adults, ADHD can cause the following symptoms:

- Inability to focus on tasks
- Trouble remaining organized and completing necessary daily chores such as making the bed, doing dishes, or washing clothes
- Impatience with people who are slower or less articulate than they are
- Difficulty reading social cues from others (e.g., missing sarcasm)
- Starting new tasks before finishing old ones
- Frequently losing items
- Having a hard time sitting still for long periods
- Dealing with forgetfulness and impulsiveness
- Inability to listen when someone is talking, blurting out inappropriate comments, or answers before the speaker finishes

A child will show symptoms like these:

- Poor academic results at school due to lack of focus on their tasks
- Behavior problems at school (e.g., not staying in their seat)
- Trouble getting along with others, including family members and friends
- Impatience with themselves or sluggish movements when they do something without being motivated to do it; trouble doing things that need to be done quickly such as assembling a toy or dressing for the day
- Interrupting others and blurting out responses
- Acting without thinking
- Trouble following instructions or routines that are laid out in a logical order
- Experiencing mood swings, a quick temper, and irritability

- Inability to deal with stress

Some adults might not have any symptoms at all while some may only experience a few of them that don't interfere too heavily in their lives. Adults might also be diagnosed when ADHD is suspected for either themselves or their children because there's no way to tell if someone has ADHD just by looking at them. The process can involve the following: physical exams, lab tests, imaging scans like X-rays and MRIs; questionnaires, and interviews with adults, parents, and teachers (in the case of adults who are still in school/ higher education, for example). There is no physical test for ADHD, but tests may be used to rule out other causes.

ADHD Symptoms in Children

In essence, there are three main (major) groups of symptoms displayed by children with ADHD: inattention, hyperactivity, and impulsivity. That doesn't mean that a child with a lot of energy or with a more impulsive character is automatically diagnosed with ADHD. As mentioned before, multiple criteria have to be met for someone (child or not) to be diagnosed with this disorder.

Many other characteristics can contribute to the diagnosis, such as difficulty sitting still or playing quietly; avoiding tasks requiring sustained attention (reading for more than 5 minutes); and fidgeting. Fidgety behavior may include squirming in their seat when they have been asked to do something, tapping items on the desk repetitively, as well as shaking their head, or wiggling in place.

For more information on the general ADHD symptoms (frequently seen in children), please refer to what has been mentioned in the first part of this chapter.

ADHD Symptoms and Your Child's Education

Since on many occasions ADHD comes with a lack of focus, it can affect a child's education. They may have trouble following instructions or recalling what was recently stated, both in the classroom and at home. This can cause them to lose interest in their work and become easily distracted by what is going on around them.

If ADHD is not being treated correctly or at all, the symptoms in children can make it difficult for them to function properly both inside of the classroom and outside of it.

Additionally, children with ADHD are at risk of growing up to be adults who don't perform well academically or at work, as well as have issues in their personal lives (such as in their personal relationships or engaging in risky sexual practices, for example). Moreover, research also shows that ADHD patients can frequently show comorbid mental health disorders (such as bipolar disorder, for example) (Usami, 2016).

This is not to say that all children diagnosed with ADHD will have these issues. It's also not meant to scare you as a parent. ADHD can be managed. Being aware of further issues is important precisely because it will help you take action now.

To help manage ADHD in children, it is important to understand what triggers symptoms. For example, when a child with ADHD enters an unfamiliar setting (such as a new classroom), they may experience significant difficulties managing their time and concentrating on the work at hand.

It's also common for them to get bored easily or distracted by things around them, and thus, lose concentration in class. Therefore, they might have trouble keeping track of what was said in lectures or following directions.

Your child needs to be taught by professionals who know how to handle ADHD. Some techniques can help a child with ADHD stay more focused, including:

- Delivering information in tidbits
- Making sure the child is seated so that all distractions are avoided
- Creating worksheets and tests that have fewer items on them
- Helping the child organizes themselves (such as by providing them with a notebook with three pockets: homework assignments, completed homework, and messages for the parents).

These are just a few strategies to employ in the classroom with a youngster who has been diagnosed with ADHD. To someone on the outside, they might not seem like a lot, but it is precisely these kinds of small things that can make a major difference in the life of someone with ADHD.

Other Symptoms of ADHD

As mentioned earlier, every person with ADHD is different. Although there might be different pathologies as to how this disorder develops, most of those diagnosed with ADHD show similar symptoms that fall into the spectrum we have already mentioned in the first section of this chapter.

In addition to the symptomatology itself, it is also important to keep in mind that ADHD symptoms can sometimes be mistaken with symptoms of other disorders, such as

- Sensory processing disorders
- Autism
- Bipolar disorder
- Low blood sugar

- Hearing problems

Of course, symptoms of ADHD should also not be mistaken with kids just being... kids. Only a medical specialist can help you find an actual diagnosis, so do make sure you visit one if you think your child might show symptoms of Attention Deficit Hyperactive Disorder.

Possible Causes of ADHD

If your child has been diagnosed with ADHD, why might be a question you ask yourself (and perhaps quite often). The sad truth is that there's no clear cause of ADHD and that this disorder might develop as a result of multiple different causes. Research is not conclusive in this respect, but staying informed will help you manage your child's diagnosis better.

For this reason, we are dedicating the third chapter of this book to exploring the potential causes of ADHD.

Let's take a closer look at this!

Genetics

According to research, genetics can play a significant impact in the development of ADHD. In fact, in many cases, it's found that children who have a sibling with ADHD will also be diagnosed with this disorder themselves (around 30% to 50%). The risk is even higher when both parents are affected by ADHD as well—they can pass on those genes to their children and cause them future problems because they are more likely to inherit an ADHD diagnosis.

This does not necessarily mean that if a parent has ADHD the child is automatically going to have the same diagnosis. However, the risk is higher.

If you have been diagnosed with ADHD in the past, genetics might have played a role in the development of the same disorder in your child (Faraone, Larsson, 2019).

Brain Development

Scientists have found that the brain develops much slower in children with ADHD and their brains get to a point where they are catching up later on when compared to other children. For this reason, many times it's not until age nine or ten before doctors can really diagnose these patients as having ADHD.

As mentioned previously, research is not conclusive in terms of what causes ADHD. However, more recent studies show that there is, indeed, a neurological basis for the development of ADHD. More specifically, studies have shown that certain parts of the brain are smaller in people with ADHD whereas others are larger.

At the same time, scientists have also learned that a specific type of neurological development that leads to ADHD can also predict when the disorder will be normalized (Singer, 2007).

Environmental Factors

While environmental factors are usually not considered to be actual causes of ADHD, they can be significant risk factors. Some of these factors include:

- Food additives and diet
- Lead contamination
- Cigarette exposure
- Smoking during pregnancy
- A low birth weights
- The neurological basis for ADHD

25

Other causes for the development of ADHD include brain damage and epilepsy. Furthermore, ADHD in adults can also be related to neurological issues that appear during their development.

How can you prevent your child from having ADHD?

Well, there's nothing specific you can do.

There are many ways to help children to avoid an ADHD diagnosis (or, better said, to avoid the progression of this disorder), but scientists have found that the best way is by giving them a good start in life as early as possible.

The earlier they get therapy and interventions for this disorder, the chances of developing it later on down the line decrease significantly. This includes things like reading with babies or even talking more about emotions and feelings while still at home so kids grow up understanding what this means.

There is no clear way to avoid the development of ADHD, just as there is no clear way to avoid the development of other mental health disorders either. What you can do, however, is pay close attention to your child's behavior and ask for the help of a specialist if something doesn't seem right.

If a diagnosis is set, the management of the disorder is key in the future development of the child. In later chapters of this book, we'll go over this in greater detail.

Chapter 2. Possible Conditions Associated With ADHD

Unfortunately, ADHD is very commonly associated with other medical conditions, both mental and physical. Being aware of these will help you better manage your child if they are diagnosed with ADHD—so we decided to dedicate an in-detail chapter on this topic.

Keep in mind that, if your child has developed ADHD, it does not necessarily mean that they will develop any of the conditions we mention in this chapter. However, it is critical for parents to be vigilant and aware of the fact that, if left untreated and unmanaged, your child's condition could deteriorate and lead to other serious medical problems.

What are these conditions, how are they connected to ADHD, and what are their symptoms?

Anxiety

Excessive worry is a symptom of anxiety, as are insomnia, nausea, heavy sweating, racing heartbeats, muscle tightness, and other symptoms.

Symptoms of anxiety include:

- Feeling restless or on edge
- Irritability
- Shortness of breath
- Trembling and twitching muscles
- Dizziness or a feeling of faintness (especially when anxious)

- Headaches
- Sweating
- Feelings of impending doom or danger

There are multiple recognized forms of anxiety, but the most commonly referred to one is Generalized Anxiety Disorder, followed closely by phobias (which are sub-categorized according to the trigger that generates the feelings of panic in the patient).

The connection between ADHD and anxiety is not fully understood. However, the way ADHD is typically expressed—by a child being hyperactive and fidgety, and constantly moving about during school, at home, or even in a doctor's office—may downplay the anxiety that accompanies the condition.

Children with ADHD are often more prone to experiencing anxieties as they feel unable to cope with the symptoms of ADHD. This sets them up for a vicious cycle of anxiousness, conflicts with others, and behaviors that intensify these feelings and compound the already difficult conditions that these children face.

Depression

In a clinical sense, depression is a state of serious depression lasting for at least two weeks. It is marked by a diminished, sad, or irritable mood. The person may have thoughts of suicide and past suicidal behavior without consciously remembering these things. Symptoms include (but are not entirely limited to):

- Fatigue or lack of energy
- Loss of interest or pleasure in activities (lethargy)
- Changes in appetite or weight loss/gain

- Sleep difficulties
- Feelings of worthlessness or guilt (low self-esteem)
- Inability to concentrate
- Difficulty remembering details
- Overthinking and overanalyzing situations

Same as in the case of anxiety, the connection between depression and ADHD is not understood at a very detailed level. It is however known that ADHD is very likely to intensify the feelings of depression.

The common symptoms of ADHD can be mistaken for symptoms of depression, and this can make it difficult to identify whether depression is present in a child with ADHD. However, in addition to the common symptoms of ADHD (listed above), children with depression may also experience fatigue or lack of energy; loss of appetite or weight loss; sleep difficulties; feelings of worthlessness or guilt (low self-esteem); difficulty concentrating; and having disconcerting thoughts and feelings that become a common recurrence.

If left untreated, children (and adults!) with ADHD are more likely to develop depressive disorders.

Learning and Language Disabilities

Learning and language disabilities are defined as conditions characterized by unexpected problems in acquiring one or more of the basic skills. These include reading, writing, spelling, mathematical calculations, and following instructions.

The disability in learning and language can affect any aspect of a child's development. It encompasses not only academic performance but also everyday activities such as engaging with people (both adults and children).

The connection between ADHD and other learning disabilities is not very well understood, but it seems that there is a relationship of causality between an ADHD child's ability to focus and how their learning and language skills develop over time. When these two conditions are present together in a child, they can be very difficult to manage as they interfere with each other's functioning and symptoms.

Gross and Fine Motor Skill Difficulties

Gross and fine motor skill difficulties are characterized by difficulties in the control of large and small muscles, respectively.

Children who have this condition typically have poor coordination, struggle to learn new motor skills, and are thus unable to perform simple everyday tasks that require the use of their hands (such as buttoning a shirt or holding a pencil).

Typically, children develop greater motor control as they progress through childhood. However, children with ADHD typically experience delays in motor development when compared to their peers.

Gross and fine motor difficulties are not as well understood as learning disabilities and language disorders etc. For this reason, the connection between ADHD and these conditions is not as well understood as the connection between ADHD and learning and language disorders.

Obsessive-Compulsive Disorder

Defined as "a type of disorder in which a person has recurrent, intrusive, and distressing thoughts and/or urges that he or she attempts to control with great difficulty," obsessive-compulsive disorder (OCD) is a condition characterized by a preoccupation with some particular activity (such as compulsive hand-washing) (American Psychiatric Association, 2021).

Children who have this condition often experience high anxiety levels when they are around other children. In particular, they may experience extreme anxiety regarding the possibility of losing the attention of others.

The relation between OCD and ADHD is not very well understood, just like in the case of other conditions we tackle in this chapter. It is however known that the symptoms associated with OCD can make it difficult for children with ADHD to focus in school and that these two conditions can intensify each other's symptoms.

Oppositional Defiant Disorder

If the conditions mentioned above are more commonly known, Oppositional Defiant Disorder (ODD) is a condition that is not as widely acknowledged these days. This disorder is defined as a pattern of behavior characterized by a lack of compliance with the demands of one's parents or other authority figures (Mayo Clinic, 2021).

Often, Oppositional Defiant Disorder symptoms are more apparent in children with ADHD than they are in other children.

Individuals who have this condition commonly get into trouble with their teachers because they refuse to follow their instructions and can only express themselves with negative comments (or even insults).

It is not necessarily easy to establish a connection between Oppositional Defiant Disorder and ADHD. Sometimes the symptoms of these two disorders overlap leading to uncertainty as to which condition is truly causing the problem.

Obsessive-Compulsive Disorder and Autism Spectrum Disorder are also conditions that are very similar to Oppositional Defiant Disorder in terms of their symptoms.

It is for this reason that it is often difficult to distinguish between these conditions.

Bipolar Disorder

Defined as a condition characterized by extreme changes in mood, bipolar disorder can be difficult to recognize in children but far more commonly acknowledged in adults (Healthline, 2021).

A child with this condition will usually exhibit two opposite behavioral extremes which are manic and depressive episodes.

The manic episodes consist of states of elevated energy levels while the depressive episodes are characterized by periods of low energy levels and feelings of despair.

These two opposite states are quite far from each other and can have a dramatic impact on the lives of those who have bipolar disorder especially when the condition is not managed.

Children with poorly controlled ADHD are more prone to acquire bipolar disorder as they grow into adults, as discussed previously in the book.

Tic Disorder

This is a condition characterized by periodic, involuntary motor or verbal tics.

The most common form of this disorder is simple repetitive movements such as blinking, nose tapping, and shoulder shrugging but different people might develop different tics. The pathology of this disorder can be quite difficult to diagnose because it is usually an unpredictable onset of these noises that are not clearly connected to other mental processes.

Tic disorders are almost exclusively diagnosed in children and require the help of a professional to properly manage. Quite often, they are also associated with ADHD because these two conditions are often characterized by hyperactivity and impulsive behaviors (Ratini, 2020).

Tourette Syndrome

Somewhat easy to mistake with the aforementioned condition, Tourette Syndrome is characterized by the use of coarse language, or chronic motor or vocal tics. It is one of the most extreme forms of this disorder as it can lead to other much more severe mental disorders such as OCD or ADHD.

Children with ADHD might also develop Tourette Syndrome though it is much less common.

Also, some people develop Tourette syndrome after having been treated for ADHD. Interestingly, studies show that less than 10% of those diagnosed with ADHD have Tourette Syndrome, but 60 to 80% of those with Tourette develop ADHD. No research points to the treatment of ADHD as being a trigger for the onset of Tourette's, though (CHADD, 2021).

Sleep Disorder

Since in some cases, children with ADHD are characterized as hyperactive, their excessive activity levels can also interfere with their sleep patterns. Along with this, they might have difficulty concentrating at school and performing the tasks required of them during the day thereby decreasing their ability to manage the symptoms of ADHD and its related conditions.

Abuse of Substances

We have already mentioned this earlier in the book but those diagnosed with ADHD are seemingly more likely to develop some sort of substance abuse as adults. The development of addiction can be emotionally taxing on the individual, but it can also further dangerously complicate the ADHD symptoms.

It is very important to note that treatment for ADHD alone might not be enough for addicted individuals and that further, specialized help might be needed.

Other Conditions Associated With ADHD

Research into comorbid conditions is not fully conclusive, so it cannot be said with absolute certainty that there is a direct correlation between them and ADHD. It is also worth noting that many conditions that appear alongside ADHD do not necessarily develop along with ADHD, but some can worsen existing symptoms of ADHD.

Chapter 3. The ADHD Advantage

Parenting a child with ADHD requires flexibility, invention, and a great deal of patience, not only with your child but also with yourself. While you will be going on to help your child using the strategies this book discusses, it is essential to realize that ADHD requires long-term management. Yes, the symptoms will improve, but the disorder will not just go away overnight. In some cases, it can be a lifelong condition. So, think of being the parent of a child with ADHD as an exciting adventure with myriad challenges, opportunities... and happy surprises!

Take Mariah, a doctor. Her child, Jackson, was diagnosed with ADHD. Mariah found it difficult to understand and empathize with his behaviors. He was clearly very bright, but he did not do the work expected of him and performed poorly in middle school. Then, in high school, he discovered the magic of physics and understood the subject so well that he excelled.

But even though Mariah did not always relate to what Jackson was interested in, she acknowledged and accepted that he would do things in a very different way than she had. So, while Mariah went directly to medical school after college, Jackson moved to rural Maine for several years to work as an organic farmer. At the same time, he took pre-med courses and eventually enrolled in the scientific research graduate program several years after graduating from college. Along the way, he made friends with a disparate group of people, learned how to farm, and brought real-life knowledge to his scientific study.

Like Jackson, many children with ADHD make surprising choices. However, if parents stay flexible and open-minded, they can support and guide their children as they make exciting discoveries about their talents and interests.

When Parents Also Have ADHD

If you also have ADHD, it may make parenting your child with ADHD feel doubly hard, but your experiences may also make you more understanding and receptive to what your child is going through. In the last several years, the world of ADHD has changed a lot. There is a much greater understanding of the condition and strategies, medications, and other interventions that help children with ADHD perform better at school and home. And for many more children are adequately diagnosed now than in years past, they can receive the help they need.

Some adults with ADHD may not have been diagnosed when they were younger, and they may have grown up without understanding ADHD or having others around them understand what they were going through. If you can relate to this, be aware that your child's experiences will most likely be different from yours; there is a greater appreciation and understanding of ADHD today. You don't need to worry that your child's experiences will replicate your own. It is undoubtedly helpful to self-reflect, but you'll want to avoid projecting any negativity from your past onto your child. The condition may be the same, but each individual is different.

If you grew up with ADHD, you likely have a greater sensitivity to your child's challenges and experiences. You may also be aware that there are benefits to having the condition. In fact, you can use your own sense of experimentation and flexibility to try out and adapt strategies to help your child.

David Neeleman, an entrepreneur who started three commercial airlines, including JetBlue, has spoken publicly about growing up with ADHD. He dropped out of college and found Morris Air, which was later sold to Southwest Airlines. Neeleman used his restlessness and sense of adventure to his advantage.

He constantly rode on his own airplanes, making sure they were comfortable and engaging to his customers. He's the smart guy who decided to install TV screens in the back of each seat because he understood that people needed to be entertained as they flew. Having ADHD made him more inventive and, in part, helped him rethink the way a commercial airline treats its customers.

Parenting Principles

As you help your child develop strategies to work with ADHD, several principles are to keep in mind. These principles will help you guide your child in a realistic and caring way, with an understanding that there is no cure-all for ADHD. In addition, the guidance you provide can help your child work at their own pace toward understanding the condition and working with it.

Practice Patience

All parents need patience, and this quality is significant for parents of children with ADHD. While it is understandable for parents to desire to "fix" their children's problems and "cure" their ADHD, the reality is that most children require time to develop. Studies conducted by the NIMH and others have shown that children with ADHD will grow in similar ways as their peers, except in brain development, where they lag behind about three years.

These studies suggest that parents can be assured that their children will eventually develop the necessary organizational, planning, and judgment skills exercised by children without ADHD. But, the slower trajectory toward maturation means extra patience, and an eye on long-term development, rather than quick fixes, may be necessary.

Keep an Eye on the Long Term

This is related to patience. Parents should understand that even though they are taking steps to help their children, they might not see immediate results. Change and maturation require time, and children may develop more slowly in some areas than in others. They may experience occasional setbacks, but these bumps in their development do not mean that they won't eventually have all of the tools they require for a rich and productive life.

Ask Others for Help

While it is normal for parents to desire to help their children on their own, raising all children, especially those with learning disabilities, truly "takes a village." In other words, reach out to a community of people who have children with ADHD, whether online or in your area, for advice and support. It is a positive reflection of your parenting style to enlist the help of adults your child interacts with, including not only teachers but also perhaps coaches, tutors, doctors, therapists, and religious leaders. Enlisting the help of others may be particularly important as your child enters adolescence, a period when children are often less receptive to what their parents have to say.

Externalize Rewards

As ADHD expert Russell Barkley, Ph.D., noted in "Taking Charge of ADHD," children with ADHD may not internalize motivation as other children do over time, and they may need external incentives and supports to change their behavior. This does not mean that parents need to bribe children.

Still, it does mean that parents need to consider what children with ADHD value, such as playing video games or sports using these interests as rewards for children's completion of more mundane activities. While many parents want children to carry out tasks just because it is the right thing to do, children with ADHD may need to be externally motivated until they can develop a more intrinsic sense of what they need to do over time. Several strategies in this book suggest external rewards to keep your child motivated.

Recognize Positive Behaviors

Children with ADHD often require constant feedback. Be sure to recognize your child is doing well, even if it's just part of a larger task or something trivial. For example, while most school-age children can get dressed and eat breakfast independently, many children with ADHD need to be praised for each step that they complete on their own—for instance, putting on their socks or tying their shoes without help, or sitting at the table for ten minutes without fidgeting.

Though many parents may feel that children should not praise children for tasks expected of them at a certain age, children with ADHD need this praise to motivate them to keep completing these tasks independently. It may feel strange to praise children who are still developing skill sets that their peers have already incorporated—or which parents think are easy—but it is necessary to keep children with ADHD moving toward independence.

Big leaps can happen in much unexpected time frames, and little changes happen all the time; are unconditionally supportive of your child, and notice when they succeed, regardless of how trivial the accomplishment may seem to you.

Break Down Tasks and Directions Into Smaller Parts

Children with ADHD often need longer tasks and directions broken down into smaller, easier-to-manage pieces. Parents, teachers, and other caregivers should avoid assuming that a child with ADHD will understand how to break down longer tasks independently. For example, in the morning, your child may need a list of each task they need to complete.

An example might look like this:

1.   Take your clothes out of your drawer.
2.   Put on your clothes, starting with your socks, etc.

School assignments need to be broken down similarly. Also, specific times for completion need to be assigned, as many children with ADHD do not have an intrinsic sense of how to plan or complete tasks within a certain time frame.

Communicate With Teachers and Other Professionals

Be open and honest with your child's teachers and other adults who work with your child, such as camp counselors. Children with ADHD have a legal right to special accommodations at school, including an Individualized Education Program (IEP), to help them succeed. However, many parents attempt to conceal an ADHD diagnosis, fearing that their child will be stigmatized.

If they are not aware of the diagnosis, teachers, and others in teaching and caregiving roles may assume a child is willfully defiant or disruptive. If you communicate honestly about your child's face, this information will help teachers work with your child. Parents should not ask teachers to excuse their children from assignments. Instead, they should strategize with teachers about how to help their child complete the schoolwork.

Avoid Comparing Children to Others, Including Siblings

It can sometimes be difficult for parents who have children with different needs and developmental trajectories not to compare their children to their siblings or peers. Children with ADHD already have an acute sense of not measuring up, and these types of comparisons, when shared with children, do not tend to motivate them. Comparisons to try to show your child with ADHD how they should behave can frustrate them further and lead to less self-confidence in working toward developing the skills they need.

Keep in Mind the Particular Challenges of Girls With ADHD

While all children with ADHD may find that their symptoms interfere with positive social interactions, girls with ADHD may run afoul of cultural stereotypes about how they should behave. For example, they may be considered odd, socially distractible, too terse, bossy, or other qualities that society—including many children, parents, and teachers—are not taught to celebrate in girls.

Take Advantage of ADHD's Benefits and Energy

While there is no doubt that ADHD presents challenges, it also can confer a great sense of creativity, high energy, and often considerable charm. The old adage, "feed the hungry bee," is a good mantra for parents. Discover what your child enjoys doing and encourage them to do it again. For example, let's say your child loves working with tools or taking things apart.

Parenting a Child With ADHD

Children with ADHD often need extra care and attention from parents, teachers, daycare workers, and other caretakers in their lives. Young children who are hyperactive need more careful monitoring to ensure they don't get themselves into situations where they might get hurt.

An older child might need some extra attention and effort to keep busy and actively engaged in things that interest her or him. A child in elementary school or middle school might need extra help in getting organized and keeping track of things, making sure assignments get turned in, and coordinating efforts between teachers and parents.

To which my question is—so what? It is almost comical how many books written for parents of children with ADHD start with the message that "parenting a child with ADHD is so very hard, you poor parents deserve a medal!" To which I say: hogwash. Also, pure unadulterated nonsense. Who said parenting was supposed to be simple and easy? Beyond that, let's not put these children into a different category of children. They're just children.

Maintaining a healthy perspective is important. The child with ADHD did not "catch" ADHD out of pure thin air. Statistically, there is a very strong probability that one or both parents, or one or more grandparents, also have ADHD (sometimes it skips generations, depending on the genetic load). If ADHD biology is part of your family's genetic history, the most constructive way to deal with it is to accept it, understand it, and take responsibility for helping the child to manage it well.

Secondly, know that most children with ADHD eventually grow up into reasonably productive and reasonably happy adults. Just like everyone else. Do not allow the disorder-mongers and mental illness purveyors to convince you that your child is somehow a different species of child, doomed to failure and unhappiness. That is also pure unadulterated nonsense.

Each child with ADHD is a unique individual, with unique strengths and weaknesses and a unique personality. As a result, each will make his or her own way in life, to different levels of success and happiness.

The goal for parents and educators is to help those children with ADHD manage age-appropriate responsibilities, learn in school, get along with and make friends with their peers, while mature along with their peers as they get older. Just like all children.

Children with ADHD need the same basic things that all children need—and sometimes they need a little more. All children need structure and routines, but children with ADHD may need them more. All children need to learn organization skills, but kids with ADHD may need to work harder and longer develop them. All children need consistency concerning study schedules, morning routines, and bedtime routines, but many children with ADHD need it more.

Developing efficient systems of organization and other productivity skills does not end when childhood ends. That is an ongoing process that lasts into adulthood for all people who care about being productive. Whether or not they have ADHD, the goal with all children is to help them build a solid foundation before they reach adulthood. Below are some strategies that could be helpful.

Maintain Realistic Expectations and Provide Appropriate Assistance

One of the leading gurus of the disorder model of ADHD decided a long time ago that children with ADHD are developmentally and emotionally delayed by an average of three years compared to their peers. This now appears to be accepted as a gospel truth by many professionals working in the ADHD field.

In my experience, this is a painting with a brush that is much too broad. Some children are slower to mature, many are not, and some are intelligent and more mature than their peers.

Some (not all) children with ADHD are slower to develop emotional self-control, but that comes with the territory of having a high level of emotionality as part of one's basic biology. Likewise, some children take longer to develop organization and time management skills, which comes with the biological territory of having a poor sense of time and a poor sense of time passage.

These are common features of ADHD biology and not necessarily "developmental delays" that cause any significant problems. As every parent knows, children develop at different paces in different areas of growth and development. It is not a race. Stereotyping children with ADHD as three years behind their peers in emotional and cognitive development is inaccurate and unhelpful.

What is important in parenting or educating any child is to take the maturity level and the skills level of that particular child. It is frustrating for all involved to expect a child to do what he is not yet capable of doing. For example, one of the most unhelpful messages to parents from educators is that "he (or she) is old enough to do that by himself (or herself) by now."

No, it is not a matter of age or maturity level. If a child needs more help to get more consistent with routines and other organization skills, for example, then provide what that child needs for as long as necessary to develop and maintain those behavioral skills.

Co-ordinate Strategies and Services With Teachers, Principals, and School Counselors

The large majority of children with ADHD do not need special education services. As mentioned above, some will benefit from more individualized attention and behavior skills training. Often this can be done on an informal basis, particularly with children in the early grades, based on discussions between parents and teachers.

If you might need a broader range of services or more structured plans, you could request to have the school conduct a formal 504 evaluation. This involves an assessment to determine the child's educational needs with input from a school staff team. Parents contribute to this process, teachers, school counselors, the principal or other administrators, and possibly the school psychologist if psychological or psychoeducational testing is called for.

Manage Clutter

Assign every object in a child's room a designated "home" location. This is where things are put when they are not being used.

The Power of Routines

All children benefit from routines to promote consistent behavior. Not every activity needs to be turned into a routine. They are most helpful for accomplishing regular tasks (e.g., brushing your teeth before going to bed) and keeping daily life manageable.

Most people with ADHD have a binary sense of time. The most urgent sense of time, and honestly, the only one that is really relevant, is best described as "now." Anything that does not fall under the current experience of "now" falls into a distant and vague notion of "later." This helps to explain why people live

45

in the moment and react to what happens next. Time does not have much "depth" to it. "Now" is the only priority; the rest is a foggy unknown that doesn't get much if any, attention.

This biological explanation does not mean that people with ADHD cannot manage time well. ADHD should never be used as an excuse for failing to plan ahead of time or being late multiple times due to a travel time miscalculation. Individuals with ADHD can do well with managing time—it just takes a little extra work.

Improving one's sense of time and managing time well can be done with the help of a variety of systems and routines. The following are some examples.

Make Time Visual

Many people with ADHD report that their sense of time improves when they can "see" time. Of course, this phenomenon helps everyone, but individuals with ADHD get an even greater benefit from it.

Using some kind of planner, hard copy, or digital is essential to making time visual. You want to be able to see your day with all the hourly time blocks and all the items on your schedule. See your week, see your month. Making time visual simply provides more perspective and makes time feel more "real." It makes planning easier, including estimating and allocating time for tasks and projects.

Learn to Estimate Time Better (The 1.5 Rule)

Two factors work against people with ADHD when it comes to estimating time accurately. Luckily, both factors can be overcome with awareness and some coping skills. First, as mentioned above, time awareness does not come naturally. It is pure biology. Second, in my experience, many people with ADHD are eternal optimists. It is part of their emotionality.

The result is chronic underestimating how long things take due to over-optimistic expectations. Sure, Merle says to herself, I can finish that paper in three hours—although actually, it will take six or more. Sure, Randall says to himself, I can get to my dentist appointment in 15 minutes—although actually, it will take 30 minutes. This explains why Merle turns in papers late and why Randall is habitually 10 or 15 minutes late. Even though it frustrates them, it keeps happening.

The solution to solving the problem of underestimating time is not to trust your sense of time. It does not matter how smart or responsible you are. If you have ADHD, the chances are that your brain will fool you, and you will underestimate how much time you need to (fill in the blank). And before you know it, your second dentist's appointment has passed you by!

An elegantly simple strategy for estimating time more accurately is to use the 1.5 rule. However, no matter how long you think you need to get something done or to get somewhere, multiply that time by 1.5. If you feel you need two hours to write that report, schedule three hours. If you think you need 30 minutes to get somewhere, give yourself 45 minutes.

The 1.5 rule works very well for people who use it daily and stick with it; it's almost spooky. The only way it probably doesn't work is when people stop using it; to work consistently, it must become a routine, a habit.

Experiences being the best teacher, some people find that 1.5 times still leaves them a bit short. In that situation, it is outstanding to convert it to a 2.0 rule. What works for you is what works for you. This principle also applies to academic accommodations, for example, when requesting extended time testing. Most people do fine with 1.5 times, but some need 2.0 times.

Time management cannot be done efficiently without using a planner. This applies to all people with a busy lifestyle, and it is critical for most people with ADHD. Without a planner, a realistic schedule, and consistent routines, people tend to be scattered and jump from one thing to another. That is the recipe for being unproductive. That old saying about inefficiency— "The best way to get nothing done is to try to do everything at once"—becomes a way of life.

Chapter 4. Effective Methods to Deal With ADHD

Grown-ups can oversee ADHD from numerous points of view. A portion of the couple is referenced underneath.

Through Coaching

Grown-up ADHD treatment includes something other than drugs. Drugs will assist patients with adapting, but they can't create abilities in individuals since they are not made to do as such. Medications may anyway make it simpler for ADHD sufferers to learn. When individuals stop their medicine, the impacts may wear off; however, intellectual abilities don't dissipate inside meager air.

ADHD instructing assists patients with learning regular ideas. They figure out how to oversee themselves much more viably in their day-by-day lives. ADHD therapy depends on the past, yet instructing depends on the present and future. Mentors for ADHD assist patients with building up their qualities instead of becoming frail. Mentors additionally help patients with recognizing the issues that they experience the ill effects of.

Mentors likewise assist patients with creating certainty so they can fend off emerging clashes absent a lot of trouble. More often than not, patients have the most challenging time adapting to their very own selves, and this is the thing that mentors do. They assist them with growing increasingly confident.

Cognitive Behavioral Therapy (CBT)

Cognitive-based therapy should be directed by either a specialist or a mentor who knows about grown-up ADHD treatment. This therapy is essential since it manages the past of a patient and causes him/her to reveal issues structure in the past that blend with an individual's present working. It may turn into a troublesome issue if past issues are not managed.

Going to cognitive therapy ought not to be considered as an indication of shortcomings. Instead, it is a positive sign that you are prepared to support yourself.

Adequate Diet

Medication, training, therapy, and diet likewise impact your condition on the off chance that you experience the ill effects of ADHD. Fundamentally, grown-ups experiencing ADHD incorporate protein in their eating routine that helps produce Dopamine. Your doctor may likewise assist you with arranging a solid eating routine on the off chance that you counsel them regarding this issue. It is a great idea to incorporate natural products, vegetables, and nuts that help increment an individual's memory, and these sorts of nourishment are not extremely overwhelming or swelling.

Exercise

Exercise doesn't mean one needs to exhaust themselves. It is only valuable to give three significant synapses a lift. Specialists have proposed that through training, grown-ups experiencing ADHD can successfully mitigate their pressure and wretchedness. It has additionally been named as extraordinary compared to other non-medicinal approaches to treat the ADHD issue.

Thousand years Medical Associates can assist you with managing ADHD when you request help.

Step-by-Step Instructions to Teach Kids With ADHD

The very idea of ADHD makes showing children with this issue amazingly troublesome. They have limited capacity to focus, an excess of vitality, and an inclination to carry on improperly without ever truly acknowledging they are doing it. Guardians and instructors have been approaching themselves for quite a long time on how to teach kids with ADHD.

Since ADHD isn't a learning issue, there is nothing about the turmoil that makes it unnecessarily hard for children to learn. This is uplifting news! That implies that if you can persuade them to concentrate on an errand, they are entirely equipped for holding what they have seen, heard, and done. The hardest part of instructing kids with ADHD is getting them to concentrate on one undertaking long enough to realize what they have to learn.

Parents, therapists, doctors, and instructors all around the world utilize the following advice on how to educate ADHD children to help us teach ADHD children.

1. **Adjust your timetable to coordinate theirs as regularly as could be expected under the circumstances.** After some time, you will start to see that children with ADHD will, in general, have a specific calendar to their states of mind unsurprising times of the day where they are particularly moldable versus times of the day where their vitality level is generally fierce. Endeavoring to design exercises during their quiet time and leisure time or physical action when their vitality is at its pinnacle will make the showing increasingly profitable for both of you.

51

2. **Break up your educating plan.** Some portion of figuring out how to instruct kids with ADHD is figuring out how to function with their issue, not show their issue to work with you. Since the greatest hindrance understudies experiencing ADHD face is their capacity to concentrate on an undertaking for any period, separating these errands into littler interims will make it simpler for them to succeed. These interims might be ten minutes, five minutes, or ten seconds, as long as they are inside the youngster's sensible abilities.

3. **Transition gradually.** Something therapists hear again and again with regards to children with ADHD is that they can't stay aware of the remainder of the family when it's an ideal opportunity to change exercises, quit playing, and come in to eat, for instance, or leave one store and travel to another. Getting things done can be a bad dream. If you can give your kid a lot of time to plan for the progress, be that as it may, telling them twenty minutes early and starting to make the essential changes five to ten minutes before you really need to, you'll see that you meet with less obstruction.

4. **Keep learning dynamic and intuitive.** One of the little-known mysteries in showing kids with ADHD—that is being utilized by guardians everywhere throughout the world (to the express objection to teachers)—is the utilization of computer games. One multi-year-old youngster with extreme ADHD had the option to figure out how to peruse on a third-grade level since he consistently took an interest in web-based gaming encounters, where perusing was a need to stay aware of the gathering. Other children react well to instructive programming that still enables them to change landscape routinely. In contrast, still, others do best have a grown-up working with them intelligently through hands-on rounds of catch, coordinating, or other expertise-building practices that don't expect them to remain in their seats.

No, reassuring children to invest unnecessary energy measures playing computer games or hopping around a room won't set them up forever spent secured away a work area. However, it very well may be an extraordinary method to show them the abilities they have to succeed and, isn't that what makes a difference most?

Figuring Out How to Listen Better With ADHD—An Act of Self-Love

One of my clients—I'll call him Jake—had an easy time making friendships as he was active, smart, and willing. However, he experienced considerable difficulty keeping companions due to his lack of listening skills. He continually meddled. He would ask something to someone and then start looking for something additionally fascinating as the person responded.

His concern was not speaking or being social, it was listening, but that was so difficult for Jake. Having ADHD made it practically impossible for him to hear someone when he looked at something that generally did legitimately intrigue or influence him.

This may sound silly; however, building up our listening aptitudes is a demonstration of self-esteem. Why? Since we pass up so much when we can't tune in! If all we hear are our considerations, we can't hear what our kid needs to explain to us or why our companion feels tragic, or when a vocation or task needs to get wrapped up. We pass up cozy connections and different delights of life.

I realize that ADHD and consistent/quick-moving musings make it hard. A few people find that drug aides and others use different methodologies to remain centered. Here are some fascinating activities to attempt. The practices beneath include mindfulness and tuning in to things we may not more often than not tune in to. They can be unwinding and charming if we approach them with interest and like a trial to attempt. The significant part isn't getting excessively disappointed if your contemplations interrupt. That is consummately typical and part of the procedure.

Practices to Improve Listening Skills

1. **Begin to get mindful of what is happening within you when another person is talking.** Is it true that you are eager, exhausted, or anxious? Perhaps you're not so much tuning in, however, simply sitting tight for an interruption so you can say something. Do you all of a sudden understand that you've been daydreaming and up to speed in your very own considerations? Do you interfere because you are afraid of overlooking what you need to say?

   See if you can understand when the listening demonstration requires less effort. Does it have to do with the person who is speaking? The clamor or the articulation of his voice? Improve when there is a passionate load on the discussion or topic? How does nature influence your ability?

   At the point when you get an opportunity, record your revelations.

2. **Develop your listening aptitudes by attempting the practices beneath**. Simply do them for no particular reason and see what occurs.

   a. Take a stroll through your neighborhood or in nature and make a promise to avoid your head and tune in to things outside of yourself. Contingent upon where you are, this could be feathered creatures, children, traffic, or hardware. It could be the hints of waves breaking or leaves stirring in the breeze. Tune in for any amazement. At the point when you discover yourself thinking, serenely note how far you've strolled and afterward return to tuning in to sounds. (It might just be 5 feet, yet that is OK!)

54

b. At the point when you won't be interfered with, tune in to a bit of instrumental music you have never heard. Possibly discover a few sites that are great assets for the sort of music you appreciate. Unwind, close your eyes, and truly tune in. Would you be able to make out the different instruments? Are there rhythms that change or rehash? Then, at the point when you discover your mind pondering, take a loosening up breath and take yourself back to the music.

c. If you get diverted or aggravated by sounds, attempt another methodology. Now and then, take a couple of moments to go to them intentionally with interest. Try not to mark them as fortunate or unfortunate; simply keep your ears open. Make an effort not to distinguish what you hear, for example, "the radiator" or "the clock." Attempt to tune in as though you have never heard anything like it and have no clue what it is. The bothering sounds may change into something intriguing, melodic, or entertaining with this sort of approach. If you can work on remaining mindful of what you hear without dissecting, judging, or giving your own considerations a chance to interrupt, you might have the option to move this aptitude to a discussion.

Chapter 5. Does ADHD Ever Go Away?

While growing up, our brains continue to develop. Still, unless the original oxidative stress is healed, the brain develops to compensate for oxidative stress rather than according to its usual design.

The ADHD brain compensates for oxidative stress rather than develops according to its typical design.

Understanding brain science can be quite complex but can be easily understood by this same concept if we apply it to a broken bone that needs to be healed.

If you have a broken bone in childhood, the bone will automatically grow back because the body is designed to heal itself. But unless the bone is appropriately "reset," according to the body's design, it will not grow back straight. By resetting the bone and providing extra protection from further injury with a cast, it not only grows back, it actually ends up more robust than it was before the break.

Similarly, recognizing the oxidative stress that causes ADHD and then "resetting" the brain with extra support to protect it from future stress, the brain can grow back according to its natural healthy design. It may even grow back stronger. Extra support physical, emotional, mental, sensory, and nutritional support can be necessary to "reset" the brain.

By "resetting" the brain, we can heal ADHD.

We must first comprehend the indications and symptoms of ADHD before we can begin the healing process. By identifying the many faces and later stages of ADHD, we can then address the cause and eventually heal the condition. Without first recognizing that we have ADHD, we are not motivated to seek out and find the answers to remedy our situation.

To make matters worse, without recognizing that ADHD is a physical condition of oxidative stress in the brain, we tend to have become overly critical of others or ourselves. We continue to misinterpret ADHD symptoms as character defects, neurosis, and/or personal failings.

With this new insight, we can view the symptoms of ADHD in others and ourselves in a more compassionate light. We can react to ADHD as we react to having a broken leg and needing to walk with crutches for a few months.

ADHD does not have to be a lifelong sentence. It can be healed. For some, this insight means they don't have to take dangerous drugs to medicate the condition. For others, it means they become less defensive about having a "disorder" or "mental condition." They are then free to focus on getting the extra nutrition their brain requires. With this new insight, the door opens to explore natural solutions to heal ADHD.

The Many Stages of ADHD

Throughout life, our brain continues to grow and develop. Complex brain changes continue into old age, which reflects our degrees of maturity. ADHD interferes with our normal development and the expression of our inner potential for success, happiness, love, and good health at every stage of life.

Let's take a brief overview of the new challenges caused by ADHD at six major stages of brain development and maturity:

- **Stage 1.** Children experience different degrees of trauma related to learning, behavior, and social challenges. The inability to excel in the

57

classroom or form supportive friendships can seriously limit one's happiness, self-image, and self-esteem, along with his or her ability to trust.

- **Stage 2.** Teens experience new social challenges, including isolation, bullying, body image, obesity, and addictions. While violence and video addiction are increasing in boys, girls are experiencing more body image problems and bullying. Boys experience late puberty, and girls experience early puberty.

- **Stage 3.** Young adults experience increasing degrees of depression and anxiety and commonly return home after college to live with their parents. More young men and women are unwilling to make lasting commitments in intimate relationships. Divorce continues to be high, shorter relationships are the norm, and there are now twice as many single people.

- **Stage 4.** Adults experience an increasing inability to manage stress levels, leading to dissatisfaction in relationships, overwhelm, exhaustion, and divorce.

- **Stage 5.** At midlife, aging adults face some version of the "midlife crisis," which includes boredom in relationships, depression based on regret, and/or boredom with work, and a longing to quit and retire.

- **Stage 6.** Elders today experience unprecedented levels of modern diseases that were previously not common, including diabetes, heart disease, cancer, Parkinson's disease, dementia, and Alzheimer's disease.

These challenges arise from the same condition that gives rise to ADHD but goes unrecognized as such.

The Unrecognized Symptoms of ADHD

As we age, our brain continues to grow and develop through different stages. At each stage, if ADHD is not healed, it continues in new and different ways. The childhood symptoms shift into teenage symptoms and so on. The symptoms of each stage remain to some degree but are overlooked or suppressed as new coping mechanisms emerge.

A coping mechanism is not always a good thing. For example, a young ADHD child may inappropriately express painful emotions. As they become older, a coping mechanism may simply be the repression of their ability to feel emotions.

They no longer inappropriately feel and express painful emotions, but they are also unable to feel and express their positive emotions as well. When asked what they feel, they feel nothing, while layers of repressed feelings and limiting beliefs are hidden deep inside their hearts. Thus, a coping mechanism is not necessarily a good thing.

Let's explore the common coping mechanisms of ADHD that may emerge according to the four temperaments.

1. **Coping mechanisms for creative children:** At puberty, children with a creative temperament who are hyper-focused on seeking new stimulation may no longer be spaced out, bored, or distracted in the classroom. Instead, they learn to cope by creating a kind of tunnel vision or focus that allows them to excel at one thing but limits their ability to enjoy other interests. They may start new projects with great enthusiasm but quickly lose interest, procrastinate, or do not follow through. They may create unnecessary drama by waiting until the last minute to finish tasks.

59

As adults in relationships, they can be hyper-focused on loving their partner initially but may just as quickly lose interest, moving on to a new partner or a new focus that provides a new challenge. They tend to be hot and cold in their relationships. They do not realize that their lack of commitment in a relationship is a symptom of ADHD but feel they have just lost that loving feeling and have no idea why.

2. **Coping mechanisms for responsible children:** A child at puberty with a responsible temperament who is hyper-controlling may stop resisting change, but they may become obsessed with being perfect as a teenager. They may become high achievers but never feel good enough. They may also become overly stubborn, rebellious, or defiant.

   They may compensate, on the other hand, by becoming subservient to the wants of others or their parents. They may become excessively vulnerable to peer pressure. As adults, they may climb the ladder of success and eventually discover they were climbing up the wrong wall. In relationships, they are often disappointed and may feel they give more and get less. They are rejected or criticized for being too judgmental or too controlling. They do not recognize that their need for perfection is excessive and a symptom of ADHD.

   They feel misunderstood because they are only trying to make things better.

   In some cases, they may cope with these symptoms of ADHD by overeating, over-exercising, or oversleeping.

3. **Coping mechanisms for bold children:** When children with a bold temperament who are hyperactive become teenagers, they may be able to sit still in class, but their minds remain busy, distracted, or bored. They may stop fidgeting, but, in their minds, they are somewhere else. It is hard for them to stay focused on a particular train of thought.

Hyperactive teens or adults may develop the coping mechanism of becoming thrill-seekers to avoid feeling bored with the routine of life. Rather than consider their "dangerous thrill-seeking" as a coping mechanism for ADHD to suppress the feelings of boredom, they conclude, "I just like to do dangerous things."

They may be unable to relax and appreciate the present moment; despite the fact that they believe this is their natural state. They are always busy moving towards some future goal but unable to appreciate what they have at the moment. Their minds keep them constantly busy thinking up new things to either worry about or achieve.

4. **Coping mechanisms for sensitive children:** Children with a sensitive temperament who are hyper-vulnerable may develop the coping mechanism of repressing their need for love and, as a result, resist or reject affection, appreciation, or intimacy.

They may become hardened by life and relationships and become overly self-reliant and independent. They always wear a smile because they are determined not to get hurt by depending on another. They can be very loving at giving but are not good at receiving. In intimate relationships, they are easily disappointed and may become moody, anxious, or depressed.

They become hardened by life and become overly self-reliant and independent. As adults, they may become overly caring for others to avoid feeling their vulnerable feelings. Eventually, the denial of their own needs catches up, and they feel alone, resentful, or hurt. Rather than recognizing over-giving as a symptom of ADHD, they may blame others for not supporting or appreciating them enough.

Understanding Coping Mechanisms

Understanding coping mechanisms help us to question and discover who we truly are. Are we simply coping with an abnormal brain condition, or are we expressing our true and authentic selves? Coping mechanisms can be so automatic that we just assume they represent who we are instead of recognizing that we may have ADHD.

In these examples, the coping mechanisms are automatic reactions, attitudes, or behaviors to avoid feeling the initial symptoms of our ADHD. They often feel good because they help us to avoid the discomfort of having symptoms of ADHD.

Coping mechanisms help us avoid the discomfort of having symptoms of ADHD. For example, if procrastination to achieve a goal is uncomfortable, a coping mechanism may be oversleeping or making something else more important and doing that. One may even decide to stay in their comfort zone by giving up their goal altogether.

When ADHD is not recognized, we can easily delude ourselves and become addicted to our coping mechanisms. Even actual drug addictions are coping mechanisms to minimize the symptoms of ADHD.

Chapter 6. Data and Statistics

Worldwide surveys demonstrated ADHD is prevalent in Higher-income-countries

According to a 2016 CDC study, there are up to 6.1 million children in the United States with ADHD or ADD. That is 8.8% of the total global ADHD percentage.

- Children with ADHD are between ages 2 to 17
- Boys are diagnosed with ADHD twice as much as girls, 12.9 % to 5.6%
- Over 388,000 children between 2 to 5 years
- 2.4 million ages 6 to 11
- 3.3 million ages 12 to 17
- The median age for mild ADHD diagnosis is 7 years
- The median age for moderate ADHD is 6 years and 4 years is for severe ADHD (Journal of American Academy of child and adolescent psychiatry 2014 and 2018)

ADHD in Teens

- 8.8% ages 13 to 14 have been diagnosed with ADHD
- 8.6% aged 15 to 16 have ADHD
- 9% aged 17 to 18 years
- Only 4.2% showed severe impairment according to the DSM-IV
- ADHD teens get more traffic violations, accidents and engage in risky driving

- 27% has comorbid and substance abuse disorder
- Have more quarrels with their parents?
- ADHD teen girls struggle more socially than boys and women with the condition
- ADHD teen boys are likely to skip school or do poorly in school work
- -10% will miss school
- Up to 8.1 times likely to dropout
- 7.5% fail their course
- Have minor GPA than normal kids
- About 2.8% of college students report ADHD or related symptoms

ADHD in Adults

- Over 2.8% had ADHD in 2018, and a 2019 report indicates it doubled from 0.43% to 0.96
- 5.4% diagnosis rate in men and 3.2% in women

The case of ADHD in children has continued to rise:

- 7.8% in 2003
- 9.7% in 2007
- 11% in 2009
- 8.8% 2019
- 11.7% of boys diagnosed in 2019
- 5.7% of girls diagnosed in 2019
- 13.6 million visits to the physician are related to ADHD
- ADHD adults are likely to get a job and keep it if it was not managed at childhood
- Likely to experience difficulty in a relationship

- Very vulnerable and likely to die from premature deaths, including accidents

ADHD Treatment

- 75% of US kids with ADHD undergo one form of ADHD treatment
- 14.9% for behavioral
- 30.3% medication alone
- 31.7% treatment for medication and behavioral

Taking ADHD Medication

- 18% of kids 2 to 5 years
- 68.6% ages 6 to 11
- 62.1% ages 12 to 17
- Currently, over 62% of kids with ADHD take medication

Undergoing Behavioral Treatment

- 59% ages 2 to 5 years
- 51% ages 6 to 11 years old
- 41.7% ages 12 to 17 years old
- 80% of ADHD have support from schools
- 40% partook in social skill training
- 31% took part in parent training
- 20% in cognitive behavioral therapy

Comorbid ADHD

- 2/3 kids with ADHD have one other condition

- 51.5% have a CD or behavioral problem
- 16.8% suffer from depression
- 13.7% have ASD
- 32.7% have anxiety
- 1.2% have Tourette syndrome
- 45% have a learning disorder
- 10 to 75% have a personality disorder in ADHD adults
- ADHD has a higher chance of losing control of eating disorder LOS-Es or suffering binge eating.
- 20% of ADHD is an adult is underdiagnosed and treated
- ADHD in adults is on the rise than in children 26.4% in children than 123% in adults
- 25% to 40% of adult ADHD suffer from substance abuse disorder
- Adult ADHD is more susceptible to drug use, including alcohol, marijuana, nicotine, and cocaine

ADHD—Race, Ethnicity, and Demographics

- Black kids aged 3 to 17 have a higher rate of ADHD, and 16.9% with learning difficulties
- 14.7% of white kids
- 11.9% of Hispanic kids
- Children from low income are 18.7% more likely to be diagnosed with ADHD than 12.7% of kids from above the poverty threshold
- More black and white children with ADHD suffer from learning difficulties than Hispanic kids with ADHD
- Parents with less than high school education are 15.4% likely to have kids diagnosed with ADHD, unlike 12.8% of kids with ADHD from parents with more than a high school education

- 41% to 55% of families with a child with ADHD has a parent with the condition
- Parents spend 5 times more to raise a child with ADHD than a typical child
- 1 in 5 ADHD students do not receive school-based intervention

ADHD Diagnosis by Location

- 11% from the south
- 8.4% Midwest
- 8.4% Northeast
- 6.8% west
- 11.8% rural settlers
- 9% urban/suburban
- ADHD by race: black 16.9%, white 14.7%, and Hispanic 11.9% respectively

Chapter 7. Accepting Children With ADHD

We all hope to bring healthy, happy children into the world that will grow up to have even healthier and happier lives. Unfortunately, genetics as well as a series of other factors sometimes leave their mark on how our children really are. An ADHD diagnosis can leave you, as a parent, feeling like you've done something wrong. It could make you feel helpless and hopeless. And, in the end, it could affect you as much as it does your child.

Before we dive into the sensitivities and details of what it means to be the parent of a child with ADHD, it is important to stop for a moment and learn how to accept this condition. Helping your child better manage the symptoms is tightly connected to how you, as a parent, manage your own reactions to the diagnosis and how you find your balance amidst the turmoil.

As such, we're dedicating Chapter 5 of the book to something that might seem simple but requires continuous hard work on your part as much as it does on your child's: acceptance.

Moving Forward After the Diagnosis

Feeling overwhelmed by sadness, anger, and anxiety once your child has received an ADHD diagnosis is perfectly normal—but it is not something you should dwell on for too long. Taking action as soon as possible and learning how to help your child manage their condition as well as how you should manage your own sensitive situation are both crucial steps you need to take forward.

The very first thing to do is learn more about Attention Deficit Hyperactive Disorder. Since you are here reading this book, it is quite clear that you are already on a good path in this respect and that you want to educate yourself more on this topic.

This is a challenging task, so don't feel like your child is the only one who has to work at accepting his or her ADHD diagnosis and its potential consequences. As you take in what you've learned about ADHD, and as you begin to understand the many facets of the condition in greater detail, you're also learning more about yourself and how well you manage stress. You are learning about your child's needs too.

Finding the right type of treatment and therapy for your child's specific needs might take time, so don't rush through everything. Try out the different options your medical specialist recommends, and always be prepared to make adjustments. There's no given recipe for the treatment and management of this condition, so you need to manage your expectations.

Do talk to other parents of children with ADHD. This will not only help you find new tactics and techniques you can use in raising your child but will also help you feel less alone in this endeavor. The community has a powerful impact on us, so surrounding yourself with people who really get what you are going through is essential.

How to Manage Emotions as Parents

As mentioned before, you might feel terribly angry at the situation. You obviously want better for your child than having to live with a disorder that will affect their lives well into adulthood.

It is normal to feel frustrated, hurt, and helpless—however; you need to learn how to manage your own emotions in a healthy way.

This can be done by finding support groups and asking for help as soon as you start feeling overwhelmed. If you are feeling depressed or anxious regularly, it would probably do you good to seek professional help. There should be zero shame in that. Just like your child, you are going through a lot of adjustments in your life, so it's perfectly normal to ask for help.

And also, just like your child, you might have to check in on your own behavior and adapt to the new life lying ahead of you. There IS a lot of hope for the vast majority of children diagnosed with ADHD—and you really, have to keep a positive mindset to be able to navigate the bursts of energy, the challenges, and the potential risks you might have to face as the parent of a child with ADHD.

Also, do keep in mind that just because your child has this condition, it doesn't mean you have to completely neglect yourself. Take care of yourself as much as you take care of your child. After all, you're not helping your child if your own mental health is deteriorating. Exercise, eat healthily and take time to get some fresh air and sunshine. Similarly, as you start to learn about the upsides of your child's condition, don't forget to search for your own positives in all of this.

How to Help Your Child Cope With ADHD

If your child is very young, they might not understand what is going on. They are just happy and energetic, and sometimes they might feel frustrated at how they cannot seem to get it right when it comes to tasks that require a bit of focus. But overall, it is extremely difficult to explain ADHD to a young child, and it shouldn't be your main priority at this time.

But you can start to talk to them about the condition as well as about their emotions, so they feel safe with you and confide in you. The more they know and understand about all of this, the better; however, again, don't expect too much from a child who is only 7 or 8 years old.

The important thing is to explain to them that they have ADHD, but that it is nothing bad: it's just something that makes them happy and energetic, just as some other children's personality is more drawn or introverted, and just as other children have blond hair.

Be honest, be transparent, guide them as you would your other children, and let them know that you are there for them.

We will discuss more the specific techniques you can use when you want to help your child with ADHD, so we will not focus on this for now. However, and this does need emphasis, do keep in mind that your child needs to accept who they are now, rather than grow up feeling that they are different in a negative way. The more positivity you can instill in your child now, the more likely it is that they will grow into an adult who can successfully manage their condition and show the same academic and professional results as everyone else.

Tips to Help Your Family Handle a Child With ADHD

There's no "ADHD parent" textbook or recipe that works for everyone. Every ADHD child is different, every family is different, and every life context is different as well—so you are most likely not going to fit into any kind of "mold."

However, some of the tips you might want to keep in mind as the family supporting and raising a child with ADHD include the following:

- Remember that your child with ADHD isn't lazy. They are just doing what is easier for them. If they seem to be hyperactive, it doesn't mean they don't want to sit still but rather that sitting still is harder for them to do.

- If they seem very impulsive, it means they are more likely to act before thinking things through.
- If they struggle at school, remember that this might be because concentrating is more difficult for them than it is for other children or perhaps the material being presented in class overwhelms them—in which case you should try and see if you can find an alternative educational scenario or a tutor who can come and help out with the academic part of school altogether.
- Make sure your extended family is very well-informed on what ADHD is and how they should behave around your child (and how they can help). Everyone has to be on the same page as to how the child will be raised and helped from hereon, so be sure that they all understand the importance of adults having the right behavior and using the right techniques with your child.
- You are not alone in this. Support groups, your extended family, medical providers can all help you navigate the years ahead of you, so that you can, in turn, help your child grow healthily and harmoniously.

Accept that your life will change. Having a child is a significant shift, but knowing that they have ADHD may make you want to be even more disciplined and focused. Your priorities will realign, your house might become a supportive place for raising a child with ADHD, and your own perspective on life might change. However, how you handle all of these changes will ultimately determine your success.

Chapter 8. Dealing With an Explosive Child

Children have a tremendous amount of energy, which is wonderful. It means they are healthy and happy and that they are doing what children do best: exploring the world and learning about it at their own pace (which, let's face it, can be a really speedy one).

Dealing with an explosive child is an entirely different affair though. An ADHD child is not merely energetic, they can be rambunctious, and what's worse, they can end up hurting themselves.

How to deal with an explosive child? Read this chapter to find out more.

Don't Worry Too Much About a Diagnosis

You will meet many well-meaning people on your child's road to diagnosis. Many will be doctors but others may be teachers, psychologists, speech therapists, and many other professionals. These are the people who, via their guidance and assistance, will be your allies in the fight for your child's treatment plan.

You could also meet some less well-meaning people including school administrators, social workers, and teachers. They may show little to no understanding of what ADHD means, and more than that, they may show little to no interest in ever learning about it.

What is important, however, is to hold your ground. A diagnosis is just that: a name on a page that theoretically helps medical professionals and therapists find better solutions. Beyond that, however, what is truly essential is to help your child get their behavior under control and show them how to manage themselves when their symptoms are flaring.

Explosive Children May Lack Some Cognitive Skills

Keep in mind that explosive children are not just overly energetic. They might lack important cognitive skills that help them regulate their energy levels, attention, focus, and learning capabilities. That is why it is critical for you as a parent to teach your child these skills and show them "the way."

For instance, self-awareness is a very important skill children with ADHD should learn.

What is self-awareness? It's the key to having a positive relationship with you. If you don't know how you act in certain situations and what triggers those reactions, it's really hard to react positively.

Expectations Outstrip Skills

Explosive children tend to have very high expectations of themselves. They tend to think they are capable of more than what they are able to deliver. As a result, explosive children regularly let themselves down as well as disappoint their parents.

The reason for this is that explosive children are often not as capable as they think and may act before thinking while lacking the cognitive skills necessary for their daily lives.

It is important to help your child manage their expectations when it comes to the skills they have and the skills they still have to work on. Of course, you want to show them as much positive reinforcement as possible, but only when the situation requires it. Do not lie to your child saying they're doing well with something they aren't, but emphasize the things they are doing well on and the things they are slowly mastering.

Figure Out Your Child's Specific Situation

Not all ADHD children are the same. Some may be more focused in certain situations; some may be completely hyperactive in other situations. Figuring out which skills your child lacks and which expectations they are not managing properly is essential for their development precisely because it will help you, the parent; guide them in the right direction.

Try a New Parenting Plan

The days of treating your child's ADHD symptoms and hoping for the best are long gone. While a diagnosis may help you identify some of the underlying causes, it doesn't simply mean that you can wait for your child to learn on their own.

Once you get a diagnosis, it is essential to figure out a new parenting plan that will bring more structure into your child's daily life. And if that parenting plan doesn't show the expected results, you should be prepared to adopt a new parenting plan. Change and adjustments are frequently required, so mentally prepare yourself for some fine-tuning in how you parent your child.

Solve Problems Proactively

Explosive children tend to be reactive when it comes to solving problems. They tend to react after they have already made a mess of things and then they explode.

What you need is a proactive solution—something that preemptively prevents the situation from reaching the explosion point and that teaches your child how to solve problems before they are faced with an explosive situation.

Prioritize Problems Before Solving Them

There is a great difference between explosive children and other children when it comes to problem-solving. Explosive children will have a tendency to attempt solving problems in a very freeform manner.

They will usually tackle all kinds of different problems as long as they are excited about doing so while neglecting other problems that could be more important or more urgent.

You need to prioritize the problems your child has and work on fixing them one at a time without allowing your child to distract themselves with smaller, less important issues or tasks.

The same applies to how you tackle your child's skills as well. Is it more important for them to make eye contact with other kids or to keep them focused for more than three minutes at a time? Focus on the things that affect your child more directly and which could have a long-lasting effect and tackle those first. Then, move on to other skills.

Don't Mislabel Your Child

Remember that your child suffers from a disorder that affects them in more ways than one. They are not just simply naughty or rascals, their brains are just not wired to focus or stay put, and that makes it hard for them to perform well in a vast array of situations (school included).

Do not mislabel your child by thinking they are simply naughty or difficult when, in reality, you may be overreacting to their situation.

If you think this might be the case, seek expert help to check if your child's ADHD is affecting more of their behavior than you think. Otherwise, you might end up focusing more on your child's misbehavior than on helping them deal with the root cause of their issues.

Get Good at Plan B

Parenting, in general, is all about being very good at making plans... lots of them, for the same matter. Parenting an explosive child means you have to be even better at building plan B, plan C, and plan D... and so on.

With explosive children, you have to be ready to adjust your plans a great deal, prioritizing what's most important and what could be dealt with easily. Simultaneously, you must ensure that these other plans are not simply rejected along the way, as they are more likely to come in helpful later. Get good at building contingency plans and build in an unforeseen problem for later on.

Don't Fret Over Disagreements

If your child refuses to eat or they throw a tantrum at the dinner table, don't worry about it. They may not be hungry and they are probably just tired. They may want to go to bed or something else and you shouldn't force them to do anything they don't wish for. Don't insist on disagreeing and constantly fighting with your child—it won't do them any good, and it will most certainly not benefit you either.

Indeed, raising an overly active child can be a challenge, but it does come with a good dose of positives as well. Focus on those whenever times get tough and then roll back your sleeves to be the parent your child needs you to be: one who knows how to guide them through the perpetually-distracting world "out there."

Possible Casualties of Parenting an Explosive Child

Staying positive is always important and even more so when you are parenting a child with ADHD. However, that doesn't mean you shouldn't be prepared for the worst-case scenarios too—which is precisely what we will discuss in this chapter. Read on if you want to learn more about the possible casualties of parenting an explosive child.

Your Relationship With Your Child

Sometimes, parenting a child with ADHD requires a bit of toughness. And other times, it requires you to be as soft as a human can be. All these shifts, as well as the rather rigid life you will organize around your child's life, can have an impact on how they perceive you (now, as well as when they grow up into teenagers, and then into adults).

Be prepared for a relationship that might not always look bright.

Your Relationship With Yourself

How you feel during the six months after your child is diagnosed with ADHD can affect how well you handle the frustration and stress of parenting a child with ADHD. The stronger your relationship was during the time leading up to diagnosis, the better your ability to overcome this adversity becomes.

There is no magic formula for forming a deep bond with your child before he is diagnosed; nonetheless, through time, you can strengthen your bond. And even more than that, you can build yourself into a stronger person (trust us, you will need this).

Do not blame yourself for what is happening. All the planning in the world cannot determine whether or not a child will develop ADHD, so there's really no reason to feel guilty over this. Practice self-love and gratitude, instead—they will be a lot more helpful.

Your Relationship With Your Spouse or Partner

We get it: parenting with ADHD often doesn't make things easier at home. You may feel like you are battling against the entire world and that's okay! Family life is never easy when there is an ADHD child in it—as we know all too well.

Make sure both you and your partner are on the same page in terms of parenting methods, behavioral cues, and techniques. Also, be sure you are both mentally strong to withstand what's coming towards you. Don't neglect your own relationship, either, because sooner or later, one of you will end up bitter and remorseful—that will not help anyone, not you, not your child.

Your Relationships With Your Other Children

Having a child with ADHD can cause some pretty dramatic changes in your other children's lives, not to mention their emotions.

Did you know, for example, that children with an ADHD sibling are more prone to develop emotional issues as well? And that includes depression!

The good news is that your relationship with your other children will be strengthened if you treat them fairly. If you can do this, then there is a good chance they will learn from your lessons and rise above the challenges themselves.

Your Friendships

It happens: out of necessity, you will be spending more time with your child than with your friends.

And while we are all for enjoying time spent with your child (it is definitely a good idea to make sure they occupy your time), don't neglect the people who love you and were there for you during the other times of the year!

Our relationships with other people are what keep us grounded, and you don't want to lose that or be left without a friend when you need them most. Take care of your friendships as much as you take care of your marital relationship and your relationship with your child. They might not seem as important in the grand scheme of things, but they are the "check-in" everyone needs—including parents of ADHD children!

The Ideas You Once Had of "Normal"

Your definition of "normal" will severely alter over the coming years, and you need to acknowledge that. Accept it as it is and embrace the "new normal," there is no other solution. After a while, you will learn to not only accept this new kind of normality but truly appreciate it as well. Because what parent doesn't love the idea of a very happy, energetic kid?

The Resemblance to the Parent You Thought You Would Be

As we have mentioned, parenting with ADHD can take a toll on you. One of the ways you can change this is by altering your perception of yourself as a parent.

Here's what we mean: to be a good parent you must be willing to do anything for your child. Even if this means going against everything you previously believed in regarding parenting techniques and strategies (e.g., play dates, consistent rules, consequences, etc.).

Your Ability to See Yourself as a Capable Strong Parent

This is one of the most important parts of your journey. You must be able to see yourself as a strong and capable parent.

If you don't, then you will have a hard time making your relationship with your child work. The only thing that can get you through the next six months is seeing yourself as the best parent possible. However, if you want to go beyond this, start by admitting that this was not something that was planned for you, and that's okay.

Be prepared for everything, because this will allow you to create plans and take preemptive actions before things get completely out of control. You have a lot of bumps in your road, and nobody can deny that. The good news is that there is so much information out there on how to be a good parent to an ADHD child! Sure, you will have to learn how to sift through the "fake news," but once you get a hang of that, you will discover the world is a pretty supportive place for people like you, so you will always find solutions to your problems.

Chapter 9. Managing ADHD Behavior Away From Home

ADHD behavior in the outside world is crucial. It can be dangerous to travel if your child goes outside limits and does damage to the property of others; the result may be costly. Even if you do not curtail the ADHD actions of your child, you risk not fulfilling your errands and upsetting strangers. When she/he handled herself/himself, it would be fine? So how can you get that to happen?

Problems in the Car

The new relationship you build with your child will help immensely wherever you go, but during car rides, certain unusual issues arise. It is both aggravating and risky to drive if your kid is misbehaving. You may be in a rush sometimes, and if your child doesn't want to help, he/she will ruin anything.

Solutions

You want your child to put on her/him seat belt without being told to do so, but if upset with something else, she/he may refuse. It makes better sense to look into the source of her/him annoyance than to focus only on her/his lack of compliance. Because the back seat can be lonely, by being proactive, you can also avoid negative attention. You can include your child in a conversation, pack items of interest to her/him, or play a game with her/him to make the trip less lonely and boring.

When driving, your child starts a commotion; you may be worried about your health. You may need to find a place for the car to rest and wait for it to settle down. Yeah, maybe you're late, but it's your best option. Let your child know, "Seeing more than one child ride with you is safe to drive, only if we sit in our seats and get along." When you return to the lane, though, make sure the kids stop fighting and do something else, even if it just looks out the window. If they are not distracted from the conflict, the fighting can resume quickly.

Who Sits Where?

When there is constant disagreement over the seating arrangement in the car, apply the same techniques that you would use to minimize conflict within the household; help the kids figure out the sharing system they want to use. Do this before your next trip: ask the kids if they have any suggestions to fix the problem at a time when everyone is calm.

Every child may have a special seating choice, but as long as the kids find out what works for them, everything is going to be fine. Make sure that their program correctly informs them, or it is unlikely to be effective, which has first preference at specific times. You don't want to keep track of whose turn it's for the seat you want.

Using the Bathroom

Trips are often long, and access to a toilet is not always easy. Your child may insist that she/he doesn't have to go to the bathroom until you go, but she may start complaining that she/he has to use the toilet shortly after she/he leaves. You should pause to comply easily but try to find a solution that reduces the discomfort if the situation is routine.

Let her/him know: "It's a long trip, and finding a bathroom will be hard. Do you want to use the bathroom now to make you more relaxed while we're driving?" If she/he says no, you might add, "We'd be happy to wait for you," as a way to make her rethink.

Help your child get into the bathroom routine before leaving—model what you'd like her/his to do and ask if like to take a turn. Then, start the journey, whether or not she/he is going. There may be a considerable difficulty if events play poorly, but try to stay relaxed as she/he pays attention to her/him own pain. She/he will eventually learn that better off modeling your actions, and you're not going to have to say a thing about it.

Problems in the Store

If you're looking for something she/he likes, your child may be very cooperative. But when she/he feels compelled to buy for others, her/his actions may be dramatically different. As is often the case, once she/he lacks the authority to determine what happens, the ADHD conduct of your child is sparked and intensified.

Solutions

If you're in a good mood, your child will behave more, so you have a significant influence. Talking about the favorite topics of discussion for your child can also help make unnecessary shopping less annoying. But most notably, if your child has more insight into what is going on, your child will probably comply more. If you're shopping for food, for example, you might ask her/his when she/he wants to help you decide what to get. Older kids might be happy to help you find bargains. Others may wish to read the list of groceries or push the cart.

The bottom line is that when you and your child get along positively and share authority, ADHD behavior will be less frequent. Try to find the "sweet spot" where you get enough space for her/his to fit you easily so that you can complete the order. This is hard to achieve, but it can be achieved, and during shopping excursions, this has the biggest long-term effect on the rate of ADHD behavior.

Resolving Public Misbehavior

When you're out and about, things may not always go smoothly, so what do you do if your child acts up? If necessary, you should disregard or avoid the actions, encouraging her to be loud and disruptive, but it is not always acceptable to others. There may also be dangers when she's/he's exuberant in public places that you don't want to play out.

Sadly, once your conduct is disrespectful or dangerous, you may have to stop your child or leave the store physically. In some situations, after a short time, it may be possible to re-enter the shop if your child settles down and you feel assured that when you return to the store, all will be optimistic.

Still, however, you might have to go back. Your child must understand that her/his behaviors have a ripple effect in these circumstances. Such adverse side effects can be illustrated. For starters, "Because we haven't done our shopping, we're going to have to go back later, and I'm not going to be able to make the dessert I was preparing for tonight."

If the problem goes on, you might want to go one step farther. You might suggest that your child spend some of her/his own money to pay for the return trip, pointing out the positives of this option (e.g., this compensates others for having inconvenienced them, and it might mitigate their complicated feelings against her/his). When she/he offers reimbursement, everyone benefits.

Like when dealing with hygiene issues, you might also ask your child if she'd/he'd like to stay home next time and use some of her/his own money to pay someone to keep her/his company. She/he thus carries some of the burdens of refusing to satisfy the family agenda. Offer her/his choices, but also let her/his knowledge that it may cost her/his some decisions.

Peer Relationships

Is your child accusing other kids of achieving a sense of superiority? Does trying to "buy" friends by giving away personal items, display low self-esteem? Should she/he whine of mistreatment in order to get you to run her/his defense? Will she/he always sit on the playground by herself/himself or just play with kids out of the familiar circle? If so, you might want to change it. You want a fun social life for your child and feel comfortable interacting with a variety of people.

Misbehaving With Peers

Often, her/his conduct becomes excessive when she/he meets another rambunctious child as a child with ADHD. If she/he behaves stupidly and doesn't try to meet standards, she/he stops feeling inferior, and when she/he plays with another cap tester, there is no loss; there is a power in numbers, and when she/he teams up with a "bad friend," your child gathers influence and leverage.

Solutions

You can try to keep your child away from other kids who act out. This can, however, give your child the impression of being weak and easily manipulated. Another approach is to make her/his realize why she/he is wrong and help her/his handle what happens when she/he faces negative influences successfully. This approach sends her/his the impression that she/he will show herself and bring about change in her/his setting. She/he will see herself/himself as a leader with good sense. You might say, "Your friend might be clever enough to imitate you when you're playing together."

You might also ask your child how she/he feels about getting in trouble and raise the question, "How do you want others to see you?" You can help her/his work out what to do when others push the envelope to find out if she's/he's scared that others will make fun of her/his if she/he doesn't join.

They may also question whether the cap checking is acceptable because the tricks may be misplaced ways of gaining attention or forms of weakening authority. Finally, let your child know that addressing her/his problem behavior with her/his peers has a crucial advantage: taking them on family excursions makes it fun.

Doubting Acceptability

If your child doubts, she's/he's reasonable to others, she/he will find it harder to act fairly. Perhaps when she/he clowns around, she/he encourages others to grin, but the unfortunate side effect is that she/he gets attention for immature behavior. She/he briefly takes advantage of habits that will inevitably not serve her/his well. If that's the case, you might say, "Do you believe you're going to have to show off or do something dumb to make people like you?" Then ask, "How is this going to work for you?" When she/he thinks it goes poorly, she/he inquires, "I wonder if there are other ways to attract them."

You want to maintain your child's great sense of humor, but you don't want her/his to be crazy or dumb. She/he has many qualities that other people will admire, and you want her/his to bring out her/his best foot. Her/his actions with ADHD diminish significantly when she/he is socially comfortable and confident that she/he is a friendly person. Additionally, her/his choice of friends will probably change if she/he feels good about herself/himself.

Supporting Social Development

If your child is young, she/he will most likely mimic many of the habits she/he observes in other adults in the household. For example, if she/he is demanding and possessive with you, she/he may also demand with her/his playmates. When family members manipulate or disrespect her/his or others give her/his a hard time, she/he can overreact or display fear. It is important to nurture habits that fit well with non-family members for these reasons. If you want her/his to communicate, accept social boundaries, and conduct with her/his peers assertively, improve her/his ability to connect within the group.

It is very beneficial to allow your child to interact with other kids while encouraging her/his social development. To increase her/his social experiences, you can promote her/his effort by saying, "Let me know when you want to bring someone over so that we can make arrangements for a play date."

Chapter 10. Raising a Child With ADHD

One of the most frequent neurodevelopmental problems impacting today's children is ADHD. It has its roots in the brain, so it's an actual neurological problem and not just a matter of bad behavior or poor parenting. That means that ADHD can be successfully treated with medication and other interventions. When raising a child with ADHD, keep the following points in mind:

- Some children can outgrow their ADHD in adolescence or adulthood, but others will always have it.
- About 10% of school-aged children have ADHD. Boys are more likely than girls to have ADHD.
- ADHD is a genetic disorder and can run in families. However, a diagnosis of ADHD does not mean that other family members will also have it. Environmental factors and not genetics play the biggest role in whether or not ADHD appears in other family members.
- Children with ADHD tend to misbehave more than other kids, making it harder for them to get along with parents, siblings, teachers, and classmates. But they don't do this on purpose—their brains just don't work right or communicate well with their bodies, so they constantly struggle to control their actions and their impulses.
- The most common treatments for ADHD are medicines and behavior therapy. Therapists who work with children use the principles of applied behavioral analysis (ABA) to help kids learn to control their behavior. The therapist rewards good behavior and ignores misbehavior—correcting it only when absolutely necessary. The goal is to teach kids new habits and behaviors that will help them succeed in school, at home, and in social situations. Medicines like Ritalin

affect the way messages move through brain circuits involved in attention span, emotional response, and impulse control.

- Treating ADHD can help prevent the disorder from affecting your child's academic performance, social development, or mental health. But it can't undo the effects of ADHD that have already been established.

- It's important to remember that ADHD is a lifelong condition, and symptoms usually get better over time. Additionally, as your child grows older and his body changes, drugs may need to be altered or replaced, necessitating new dosages.

- Kids with ADHD will always have some behavior that others don't like, but parents can help them negotiate social situations by teaching kids how to wait their turn and give other children fair treatment. Parents also can teach their children new ways to act when they misbehave so they aren't always punished for it. Kids should know that it's okay sometimes not to listen or wait your turn. What matters most, though, is that they learn to follow the rules. You can help your child with ADHD make good choices by showing that you're not angry when he does something wrong, and don't treat him any differently than other children.

- ADHD is a disease, which means that it's manageable even if it can't be cured. It's vital to remember that children with ADHD are just as unique, intelligent, and competent as anybody else. Parents who are willing to work together with teachers, doctors, and therapists can find effective treatments and ways to help kids overcome their challenges.

Games for Explosive Kids

Water Color Painting

Once your toddler reaches 24–30 months old, he or she starts recognizing and appreciating colors. It is, therefore, fitting for toddlers to be exposed to painting activities. The materials needed for painting are cheap and readily available in stores so it will not be difficult for parents to set up a small corner or outdoor area for painting.

Before you leave your child to paint on their own, make sure to establish clear rules. First, demonstrate how to properly handle the materials. Second, show your child where to hang their finished painting. Lastly, show your child how to clean up after. Take note all these demonstrations are just done through modeling. You do not even need to speak a single word. Just show your child how it is done.

Playing Musical Instruments

While most activities are performed with either the left or right side of the brain, music engages both sides of the brain, strengthening your child's ability to multitask.

If your child is musically gifted, encourage them by signing them up for lessons, investing in the instrument of their choice, or whatever else they need to pursue their passion. Singing groups, orchestras, and choirs are also an excellent way for your child to improve social skills and make like-minded friends.

Aside from the interest in colors, older toddlers are very sensitive to musical notes which make it the perfect time for them to be introduced to different musical instruments. Some child-friendly instruments are child-sized organs, tambourines, mini-guitars, and mini-drums.

Similar to how you introduced painting to your child, make sure you demonstrated well the proper usage and storage of the instruments. Show how to gently press the keys, gently strum the strings, or gently tap the tambourine to not create a loud noise. Keep everything orderly and manageable.

Once your child knows how to properly use the instruments and how to properly stow them away, let them play the music that they want. Even if it sounds incoherent to you, for your child it is already a good melody. Prevent yourself from correcting your child except when they mishandle the material; instead give praises when they do the activity in an orderly fashion.

Individual Sports

Your child may find team sports challenging because of their disorder explosions symptoms, so you might want to consider individual sports instead of helping your child succeed better.

If your child is a sports lover, they have dozens of exciting and enjoyable individual sports to choose from, such as:

- Martial arts
- Tennis
- Wrestling
- Swimming
- Bowling
- Fencing
- Table tennis

- Skateboarding
- Roller-skating
- Ice skating
- Track and field

Your child's natural high energy and enthusiasm will help them succeed in these types of sports and even become a champion!

Likewise, if you feel that your child's abilities are perfect for a particular sport, again, don't pressure them if the sport isn't appealing to them. Let your child suggest and choose.

Whatever individual sport your child chooses to practice, it will be a perfect outlet for their energy. It will help keep disorder explosions symptoms in control, help them focus better, develop social skills, and sleep better.

Indoor Activities

When the weather doesn't allow for outdoor activities, you need to have various indoor activities to keep your child occupied and give them an outlet for their energy. Ideally, indoor activities should follow these basic rules:

Indoor Activities for Kids With Disorder Explosions Need to Be Structured

Those kids crave structure. They need to know what will follow, what to expect, and how they are supposed to act in each situation.

What will I do? Where will I be? What is okay for me to say or do?

You need to provide that structure for them in the form of structured activities. That means telling your child what he or she has to do, providing the required materials, and making it clear what they need to do to win or succeed. An example is telling the child to color in a whole page of a coloring book using three colors.

Indoor Activities Should Involve as Many Senses as Possible

In the above example, you have engaged the child's sense of touch and sight.

Multisensory activities help the child focus better. Some multisensory activities include:

- Cooking
- Board games
- Card games
- Building with Legos
- Hula hooping
- Coloring and painting
- Play Dough
- Twister
- Jumping rope
- Balloon volleyball

Indoor Activities Should Involve Movement

Of course, this is not always possible with all games. Gauge your child's energy and mood and decide whether you need to structure the activity with more (or less) movement. Or, combine activities with more dancing activities, with quieter activities like board games or video games. Remember to structure time for these activities as well.

Indoor Activities Can Be Group Activities or Individual Activities and Activities With More Movement and Quieter Ones

Here are some more suggestions:

- Hide and seek
- Dancing
- Charades
- Baking cookies
- Building
- Listening to audiobooks
- Crafts
- Scavenger hunts
- Singing
- Obstacle course
- Tramp lining

Now that you get the idea, go ahead and come up with some activities of your own to ensure that your child stays active and engaged on those rainy days!

Play Therapy

Play therapy is a fantastic tool. It is used in many psychotherapy and child psychology areas to help children with disorders develop skills while having fun.

You may choose to have your child engage in play therapy with a specialized child psychologist; however, you can easily use this method with your child at home as well.

Art Therapy

This type of therapy helps children develop their creative talents and express themselves through art. The child is asked to make a painting or drawing, describe their day at school, or an enjoyable event, something they like, or even draw themselves as they feel.

The child's artwork may uncover specific issues that he or she is having, allowing parents or the therapist to discuss them further. Besides, it's just a great way to keep the child-focused while exploring and developing their creativity and uniqueness. Here are some suggestions:

- Making a collage with old photos or pictures from magazines.
- Designing a postcard with a short message to someone the child is angry with or wants to thank.
- Making a digital slide show with photos that make the child happy (or sad)
- Responding to music; listening to a short piece of music and drawing how it makes the child feel.
- Decorate a window with window markers
- Write a message to a balloon and send it flying away.
- Finger painting
- Drawing a self-portrait
- Making a drawing for someone special
- Drawing with eyes closed

The more challenging forms of exercise result in better brain function. Jujitsu, taekwondo, judo, karate, and other similar martial arts sports challenge both mind and bodywork very well for children with disorder explosions. They teach your child to focus and concentrate. They sharpen memory through their series of actions. They help develop excellent motor skills. They teach timing and balance. They also help your child realize that actions have consequences.

Other forms of exercise that have benefits similar to those of martial arts include dance, yoga, gymnastics, and rock climbing.

Fantasy Play

Children with disorder explosions often have trouble expressing and channeling their emotions. Fantasy play is crucial for teaching kids with disorder explosions how to express themselves better when feeling angry or frustrated.

How to structure play therapy?

- **Set fixed times.** Play sessions should be between 10 to 15 minutes so that the child does not get bored; however, if the child retains an interest in the game for longer than that, allows him or her to continue.
- **Prompt the child while playing.** For example, if you are playing with a puppet named Fred, start the game by saying, "One day as Fred was walking to school..." or "Once upon a time, there was..." During the game, you can also prompt your child by playing a role in the game.
- **Encourage good social behavior during the game.** For example, "What will happen if the doctor shouts at the sick person?" or "How will the little girl feel if her friend doesn't want to share?"

Some suggestions of fantasy play are:

- Playing with dolls
- Doctor kits
- Han and finger puppets
- Stuffed animals

- Action figures and monster figures

Learning Life Skills

These skills are crucial to developing at this age as they will remain with your child for life. They include learning to handle frustration and anger, wait their turn, and finish assigned tasks. Games that help build social skills include:

- Let's go fish
- The memory game
- Chutes and ladders
- Chinese checkers
- Clue
- Role-playing with costumes or masks
- Playing with action figures
- Mock tea parties

Play therapy for older kids:

- Strategy video games
- Time management video games
- Superhero role play
- Art therapy

Brain Games

Researchers from Kennesaw State University and Augusta State University in the U.S. have shown that brain games can be a new form of disorder explosions therapy. Brain games stimulate the prefrontal cortex of the brain and help explosive children overcome distractions. The study suggested that brain games could be an alternative to medication. Following studies have concluded that brain games work to develop the brain, improve focus and attention, and help disorder explosions kids learn better. The ongoing research is very promising.

Following these findings, dozens of "brain training" programs have emerged, many of them making huge claims that are not backed up by science. My advice is to beware of these programs and stick to traditional brain games like puzzles, riddles, and brain teasers. Do not shell out money to a bogus program.

Brain games benefit children with disorder explosions by:

- Strengthening memory
- Developing problem-solving skills.
- Enhancing logical thinking and deduction skills
- Improving concentration
- Promoting pattern recognition
- Video brain games improve visual perception and spatial recognition.
- Enhancing cognitive skills.
- Enhancing reasoning skills.

Brain games help children learn these skills by having fun, which is always the best way to learn. Therefore, it makes total sense to schedule these types of games into your child's activities.

Here are some good suggestions:

- Brainteaser eBooks.
- Brainteaser websites
- Riddle eBooks

- Video brain games
- Crossword puzzle books
- Logic problem books
- Brain game apps. There is a variety to choose from suitable for all ages.
- Additional activities and fun games

Coloring Books

Coloring books have been around since our grandparents' time and are generally overlooked in today's digital era. However, the benefits of coloring for your explosive child should not be ignored. Children are never too old to color, and in fact, paint has been shown to relieve stress in adults! The benefits include:

- Preparing preschoolers for school
- Improving motor skills
- Developing good handwriting
- Enhancing creativity
- Developing awareness of colors
- Improving focus
- Improving hand-eye coordination
- Enhancing confidence when kids are praised for their work.
- Developing self-expression skills.

Drama

If your child loves to act and has the talent, drama groups and classes will benefit them immensely. They will have to focus on memorizing lines and learning to interact with others in a group effort within a structured environment. To top it all off, the applause at the end of the show is just the kind of praise and encouragement he needs!

Debate Teams

That could be a very fun learning experience for your teen. It will sharpen his communication and social skills, challenge their intellect, and showcase their natural enthusiasm and passion. It can also lower their stress level and bring out their best self. Join a local, state, or national debate team. The majority of debate programs are student-run and student-operated. As a team, they will have to follow the debate rules. They are familiar with making directed speeches to a large audience. They write and share their prepared speeches. They are used to being creative and are sometimes even artistic in their speech delivery and argument style.

Playground and Obstacle Games

Bringing your toddler to the playground is one way to take away their home boredom. Introduce your toddler to the various obstacle games present in the park or playground nearby. Always demonstrate how to perform such courses for safety. Let your toddler experience the tire game or the balance beam, but of course with your close supervision. Let your child experience other obstacles courses as crawling under arcs and the like. This will not only improve your child's physical strength, but it will also improve his/her thinking skills as well as his/her patience and determination.

Outdoor Chores

Toddlers love to sweep. You will be surprised by how much patience and exactness they have in using the broom and the dustpan. If you have a huge lawn with dried leaves, bring your child out to the yard and demonstrate how to sweep the dried leaves. After a few demonstrations, give your child a child-sized broom and dustpan and you'll enjoy your toddler go.

The first 5 steps in transforming an explosive toddler into a calm one are long-term solutions as well as forward-thinking remedies to temper tantrums. These 2 steps do not wait for the toddler to throw a fit; instead, it helps prevent the frequency of tantrum episodes. Since these two steps are long-term solutions, their implementation requires time and consistency as well. With enough patience and love, both steps will reap rewards in the future and will help reveal a calmer toddler sooner than you think.

The remaining 2 steps to transforming an explosive toddler into a calm one are more short-term and will show immediate results. Even if it has short-term effects, all steps must still be carried out consistently so your toddler will know what to expect every time he or she throws a tantrum.

Assume you are trapped within a video game, where everybody is coming at you simultaneously. Every sound, sight, and sensation serves as a deterrent. Getting through a regular day for a youngster with disorder explosions is similar to that. It also explains a lot about how they perceive the world.

Lack of concentration, impairment of functions like impulse control, memory, processing speed, and the good at following directions are common symptoms of disorder explosions in children.

For years, it was assumed that all of us were born with an abundance of brain cells; but we have been unable to generate more or modify how those cells functioned. Neuroscientists have found the presence of a phenomenon known as neuroplasticity, which allows the brain to create new cells or change the functioning of existing cells.

Cognitive exercises or games have been shown to generate desirable changes in how the brain functions and appears. This implies that parents may now work with their children to assist them in improving their explosive disorder symptoms.

To get you started, here are a few basic games.

The Memory Game

This game is really simple yet extremely effective. It significantly improves the memory and attention span of children with disorder explosions. The memory cards are arranged face down on the table. The first player takes two cards and tries to match them. If the cards do not match, the player must reshuffle the deck and place it face down. To recall where the card was put, the kids must keep their attention on the cards at all times.

Chutes and Ladders

This game is not only entertaining to play, but it also teaches vital lessons about predicting success and dealing with loss. The game's goal is for the players to proceed along a path that leads to the top of the playing board. You climb ladders (the success part), and if you fail, then chutes slide down along the route. When the children have to slide down on the chute, they become agitated, but they immediately realize a ladder nearby. Failure leads to success—this game teaches valuable life lessons.

Hoot Owl Hoot

This game is primarily about forming bonds with your teammates. Hoot Owl Hoot's goal is to get all owls back to their nests well before the sun rises. It is a battle with the sun. The players take turns choosing cards and deciding what steps they should take. Each action has a rationale, demonstrating that executive functioning abilities are honed throughout the game.

Battleship

Battleship is a strategic board game in which one player attempts to sink the ships of the opponent. This board game is fantastic for disorder explosions kids since it teaches them how to think logically and reason. It exposes kids to grids and coordinates, which incorporate basic arithmetic concepts.

Chess

Chess has long become one of the most popular disorder explosions games and one of the finest games for concentration. It not only improves attention but also helps to enhance strategic thinking abilities. You can play it as a board game. The main goal of the game is to checkmate your opponent. It is played on an 8x8 grid with each opponent having 1 Queen, 1 King, 2 Bishops, 2 Rooks, 2 Knights, and 8 Pawns. Each piece moves distinctly; chess pieces are generally black and white, and white always moves first.

Sudoku

There are several stages of difficulty in the game. According to these levels, the game will begin with numbers that have already been put in the grid. Not only does this game increase attention, but it also helps with math, focus, concentration, learning, and memory. So, if you are searching for activities to help explosive children enhance their focus, try Sudoku.

Chapter 11. Guidance for Parents

Start by asking yourself what kind of family you want to have. What are your core values? What do you want to teach your children?

Do they need discipline or are they better suited to privilege and learn as they please? What are the boundaries in your house? Are gadgets out or restricted after a certain time period, before dinner, or only on weekends. Do electronics need to be put away at certain times for the sake of reading and conversation? Do computer screens need a break from intense use for the sake of healthy eyesight (at least 20 minutes every hour)?

Limit screen time is a topic that many parents struggle with. This is an area that you want to be open to discussing with your children and their pediatricians or eye doctors.

The AAP recommends no screen time for children under the age of two. Even the best content in the world will not make for the healthy development of a human being under two. The AAP also recommends no screens in bedrooms and even recommends limiting the use of screens at meals—having food, conversation, books, play, etc., in a different time slot than electronics use.

Start here: Let go of any guilt you have about screen time; you don't have to feel like a bad parent if your child is using a device more than you like—just resolve to plan ahead with what you allow and why and when.

Plan Bedtime Routine

Have a set bedtime and make it early enough for kids to get sleep. Have the same amount of awake time in the morning as you do at night. Make sure your child's day includes exercise and outdoor play. Is your child eating breakfast, lunch, and dinner? It's a good idea to reduce sugary snacks or eliminate them completely. Do you have a plan for helping him/her sleep through the night if that is an issue? If your child is having trouble sleeping at night, try these tips first:

1. **Consistency**—set a consistent bedtime and take away all screen time at least one hour before bedtime. The bedtime routine needs to be the same every night so your child knows what's coming.

2. **Establish a positive sleep association**—do not let them fall asleep viewing screens or using electronics because then they will associate their devices with sleeping—this is not a healthy relationship.

3. **30-minute wind-down**—start 30 minutes before bedtime. Dim the lights, and make sure it is quiet. Try listening to some relaxing music. It also helps to have a storytelling session before your child goes to bed.

4. **Make their room calm and dark**—if your computer screen makes their room too light, consider getting blackout curtains for that room or for the entire house (they can be found at Target and Walmart). You can also create a calming environment with:
   a. A fan;
   b. A lamp that does not emit light or a nightlight;
   c. A lavender-scented room spray or lavender-scented bed sheets;
   d. A calming activity like "the wave," "the turtle," or, more challenging, but more thoughtful and present, storytelling.

See more here: Asking Your Kids to Sleep Together (Floating Apps) and tips on the page for parents. If your child is struggling with sleep, talk to your pediatrician about possible issues like adenoids, allergy issues, or hormone imbalances.

e. Say goodnight to your smartphone

It's a good idea to put your screen away at least an hour before bedtime. Have a technology curfew and tell your kids why you are doing it and how it will help them be healthier. Do you want to be the family that eats together, watches TV together, or plays board games? This is an opportunity for you as a parent to model for your children what you want as a family value and what you are valuing in their lives.

Everyday Limits for Parents

- Do not use the screens in the bedroom.
- **Turn off all devices 30 minutes before bedtime**—or even better; put them outside of hearing distance from the bedroom (in another room).
- No screens in the bedroom after waking (no matter what device)
- Offer toys and books to encourage social play.
- **Bedtime rituals**—at bedtime, get all screens out of sight and turn off, or put them in another room. If your child is younger, this gives you time to help him or her fall asleep. Wait 30 minutes before turning on any screens in your child's room.
- **No devices at meals**—take it outside! At least 20 minutes—and keep having a meal together to build family time together with no tech distractions. Eat with the family and then have time for a quiet

conversation about whatever you want, just not in front of the TV or computer screen.

- Offer your child quiet toys and books to play with at mealtime.

- If you have a smartphone, but the battery is in and sticks it in a drawer every night. This is a good place to store your cellphone if it's not in use—especially if your child is fewer than two.

- Do not let screens be an easy source of entertainment or an easy source of interaction with people or other characters online. If your child asks "how do I..." on any number of topics that would be easier answered by a tutorial or book, tell them to ask the question in person when they are older and can take advantage of a library, museum, or another technology-free resource instead.

- **Limit exposure to YouTube**—this is not a healthy relationship. It is no longer an option for children under two. Instead, encourage a TV-free home and support the creation of technology-free environments for your child's learning and development. The American Academy of Pediatrics recommends screen time in their house be limited to one hour a day—or less; they recommend you start with no devices at all, because it's such a powerful habit that it's easy to get comfortable with screens very quickly, making it hard to have them out of reach once you've started using them. The AAP confirms that the more we use screens, the more our kids use them. They also confirm that factors like sleep and exercise often play a big role in development.

If you want to be a positive influence, remember these strategies:

1. **Stay involved**—choose when, where and what your child uses technology for. Don't succumb to peer pressure or let others make decisions for you or your child.

2. **Keep it all private**—this includes social media accounts, lovey threads (like private Facebook chats), photo albums, and any other private messages between parents about your family's technology habits, including conversations about screen time with other family members.

3. **Keep it all in the room**—if you are using your device, use it without calling anyone or texting anyone. Turn off features like location tracking and automatic Wi-Fi connection.

4. **Keep your child's data private**—turn off tracking on their apps, keep your passwords private and make sure that the apps they use are secure.

5. **Keep family conversations normal**—talk about what is happening in your house, whether good or bad, as you would with a friend or a colleague, and be open to listening to each other when you disagree.

6. **Stay positive**—see this as an opportunity for your child to say a big "yes" to learning and growing up in the tech world. It's not your job to be their friend, but it is your job to create a healthy environment for them.

Connecting With Kids Around Screen Time

Here are some ideas on ways to chat with your kids about screen time and get a better understanding of how they feel about it:

1. **Ask them questions**—"Why do you think that is?" or, "How do you feel right now?"

2. **Ask them to tell you their stories**—"Can you tell me a story about how you got stuck on that level in the video game?"

3. **Hang out**—turn off the screens and play with your child or go and connect while they're out, or let them do it together. This is a great

opportunity to build, as well as a disconnect - it's great to socialize and be honest but not at the same time.

4. **Keep it simple**—encourage this behavior, but remember that children tend to get bored very quickly and that being constantly attached will not always be healthy for them.

5. **Make it a habit**—make screen time a normal part of your family's routine and just like any other routine, remind your child that it is for brief periods and then it is over. You can talk about some rules in advance to help make this easier.

The Bottom Line

Technology use isn't inherently bad, but the lack of parental involvement around tech use and the potential for overexposure to technology has become an epidemic. We now know that children will get overstimulated by screens because they stimulate parts of the brain that are already being stimulated— so they offer no real value as stimulating environments when parents aren't around. In fact, they displace meaningful time and limit opportunities to grow healthy relationships with peers and family members. With overuse, thinking can be impaired as can learning, sleep, and body development.

We now know that children need to learn how to regulate their own use of technology. Babies don't come with an operating manual—you have to teach them how to play by putting down the screen and guiding the device down the hall or out of the room when it's time for screen time to end.

Impact of Explosive Disorder on Education

It is common to have an educational and learning impact with the explosive disorder. The classroom is another area where those explosions can be detected, and when brought to the doctor's attention, it can provide a more accurate diagnosis for the child, apart from what the parent has observed at home. When it comes to the classroom, challenges faced by the growing child include learning impairments and restrictions that affect their academic ability. Other issues that could show up are also limited reading capabilities, limited calculating and writing skills as well as sequencing movements. The child could also have trouble doing general tasks, they can also have interpersonal issues relating to their peers, playing with their peers, and having an interpersonal issue with friends and authoritative figures.

Academic and education problems are often the signs recorded in research and studies of explosive children. While the symptoms such as impulsivity, lack of concentration, hyperactivity as well as intermittent aggression are less severe, it is still to a high degree when compared to children without the behavioral disorder.

These studies also show that when these children come into adulthood, they fall into these main groups:

- Most of these children have limitations in learning and applying their skills and knowledge
- They have sustained functional impairment
- They also have constrained social participation
- In the end, around 25% work in parallel with those without ADHD
- Less than 25% of adults end up developing substantial problems.
- To date, it is unclear what factors contribute to the long-term outcomes of disorder explosions.

Chapter 12. Choosing a School for Explosive Child

For students, behavioral disorders may be a challenging issue. It impacts a child's capacity to focus, concentrate, and give their all-in academics. If a youngster is hyperactive, he or she may find it difficult to sit still, becoming restless and uncomfortable in the process. Some children cannot resist their need to speak at inopportune moments, interrupting the learning process for the rest of the class.

Despite the difficulties, schools may develop programs and processes to reduce distractions and assist these children in focusing on their work.

Here are 6 pointers to help you choose the appropriate school and programs.

1. Find out more about your child's learning preferences.
    Before you select any school, you must first understand your child's personality and academic problems. Here are a few questions to ponder.
    a. Is it easier for them to learn or recall things if they can touch them?
    b. Is it true that your youngster learns best when they are moving?
2. Take note of the structure. Explosive students require daily organization and consistency. Because there are defined expectations and processes, this framework can serve as a basis for learning. It enables pupils to focus on a single piece of information simultaneously instead of a string of data.

3. Determine the student-teacher ratio. The average student-to-teacher ratio is 16 to 1. The school you pick should, at the very least, mirror the national average. However, when it comes to explosive pupils, the smaller the ratio, the better.

4. Many parents might feel their responsibilities end at home with the kid, and that the teacher is who should deal with them at school. Parents, on the other hand, have a larger part in their children's education than simply dropping them off at school and attending PTA meetings once a month. Admittedly, teachers do play a very big role in the child's life, especially differently-abled ones.

5. Work with the child's teachers and others to help your child control the disorder and get as much from the school experience as possible. Allowing your child to perform well at school is a big part of coping with behavioral disorders in children. For your child to flourish at school there must be collaboration between the teachers, school administrators, and the child's parents. Teachers should be well-informed about the child's condition so everyone can be on the same page regarding his needs.

6. It is also essential to let the teachers and school officials know that you have expectations for your child as far as his education is concerned. Make it clear what your goals and objectives are and work with them to achieve them. Get input from the teachers regarding how reasonable those expectations are and welcome their advice and recommendations but are alert for signs that the school has given up on your child and speak to the teachers about it right away. If both teams are not working in tandem, the child will not flourish in that atmosphere.

Teaching an Explosive Student

You may be wondering if your child's teacher is doing all that they can to support your explosive child's learning journey this is a common concern. Plenty of parents may be wondering it can be both hard for a teacher and a parent, and often, the collaboration between parent and teacher can determine the success of the child's coping skills at home and in school as well as their success in life. Teachers, after parents, have a critical role in the lives of students, and when behavioral disorder solutions are used in the classroom, it can demonstrate to the child that they are valuable and capable, which the child will believe, and great results will follow.

You may be a parent reading this to know what a teacher can do in school, or you may be a teacher exploring ways to help the explosive student in class whatever it may be, here are some effective strategies that can guide both parent and teacher to establish a structured and supportive classroom inclusive one, encourages learning, enforces discipline and boosts self-esteem.

Making Rules and Routines Are a Part of an Explosive Student's Life

It is just not at home that rules and routines are important. Set short, simple rules in the classroom with student feedback. Again, positive reinforcements and feedback are essential. Instead of saying no, you cannot do this, or no you cannot do that, give students an outlet, or a template of what is expected of them. You can say, "When you get into a class, check the board for your assignments before you do anything else," or you can say, "When you enter class, speak only when you have settled in your desk." Your instructions could also be "Find your seats first and then you may talk quietly with your friend. When I start teaching, the conversations need to stop."

Establish Classroom Sequences

Doing so will help stay on task for explosive students. Some of these routines include having Row Captains that are in charge of making assignments is collected at the end of the day. You can also make it a point for explosive students to check in with the teacher or with a peer or Row Captains to see if the assignment is understood and if there's anything that they may need to clarify.

Give Appropriate Supervision to Explosive Students

We need to make one thing clear; explosive disorder is not a learning disability, like dyslexia, for example. This disorder makes learning difficult. It just makes it hard to learn something when a student struggles with focus and concentration and to focus on what the teacher is saying, and when they also cannot sit down and pay attention.

School Options for Children With the Explosive Disorder

The explosive disorder gets solved through learning. You can't absorb information or get work done if you're experimenting with the classroom or zoning out of your immediate environment.

Understand what the school requires children to do; sit down; listen; concentrate; adhere to instructions; focus. They are things explosive children have trouble doing, not because they aren't prepared, but because their brains won't let them. But that doesn't mean that those kids can't do well in school.

There are several things parents and educators can do to help explosive children thrive in class. It begins with analyzing each child's weaknesses and talents, then discovering creative techniques to help a child focus, stick to a task, and work out how to explore their full potential.

Relationship Between Explosive Disorder and Learning Disabilities

When we learn, our brain involves various executive functions, especially the elements that concern paying attention, focusing, engaging in a task, and using working memory. Through research, we also know that explosive disorder affects the brain's executive functions. For many people struggling with a behavioral disorder, learning, and schoolwork are a challenge because it involves these executive functions, but they do not have enough of an impairment to be diagnosed with LD. Suppose a person has signs of explosive disorder and LD together. In that case, this means that he or she has significant impairment in executive functions along with the loss of the specific skills required for reading, writing, and mathematics.

Expose Explosive Children to High-Interest Literature

One of the best ways to help an explosive child who struggles to read is to give them books on subjects that interest them. Some children like dinosaurs or trains; they may like elephants or even unicorns, pandas, Peppa Pig, or fairy tales. Giving children books related to the topics that interest them can help them do a better job recalling the text they read. You can teach your students how to become active readers by also teaching them various literacy strategies. For those students, maintaining attention to stories and passages that are stimulating, exciting, and shorter has a higher success rate.

Teach Active Reading Strategies

Active reading strategies can be taught to your students and even those with reading difficulties. These strategies are:

- Underlining texts and words.
- Taking and adding little notes to words that are hard to pronounce.
- Using colored pencils to mark syllables.
- Using highlighters to highlight new words.
- Post it to jot down important points to remember.
- Using colors to highlight phrases and passages.
- We are using icons like stars and circles.

If the student cannot write tips and notes in the book, the parent can get a second-hand copy of the book or, if allowed, make a copy of the book so the student can highlight, make notes, underline, circle, and write on their reading material.

As an educator, you can walk the student through this reading process and explain to them the various strategies they can use, how vital highlighting is, and how to make sense of the words together. This guided practice should be done at all reading sessions to develop students' competence with "Active Reading" skills.

Preview Content to Improve Reading Comprehension

You are previewing materials before reading and it is always a good idea for explosive students and even students with dyslexia. Both teacher and student can list essential information in the reading material, which appears on the passages. As a teacher, you can also provide general information about the reading topic, the characters, and the setting to give the students some head start.

Before the student reads a passage, follow him/her through several summary techniques by looking at the title, headings, diagrams, bold or italicized words, sidebars, and questions. You can also discuss how the reading material is arranged in its sequence.

Provide students with instruction in finding introductory and summary paragraphs. Using story maps or mind maps to help students recognize the main components of reading material and arrange them is also an ideal way to make reading easier.

Reading Aloud, in Silence

The subvocalizing technique is also an excellent tool for reading. In contrast to silent reading, it means speaking words while you read aloud but softly. The point here is to subvocalize as if you are reading it aloud, but just reading it softly. In other words, other students are not able to hear it. Reading aloud is a great strategy buff for some; it just slows the reading process. Silent reading can be difficult for children with problems with attention. The input from subvocalizing often helps these students to concentrate on the text.

Use Monitoring Methods

Teaching students techniques for monitoring their reading comprehension is also a great way to improve reading. Getting them to practice paraphrasing, summarizing paragraphs, asking questions, and even making predictions about what may happen in the story are all part of monitoring. It also helps create better clarity on the reading material.

Allocating More Time to Read

As with dyslexia, they are giving disorder explosions students extended time for reading and it is beneficial. For many students, their main issue is working memory and slower processing of information speed. So, they would greatly benefit when additional time is given to read and comprehend their reading materials. Not only that, but the extra time also gives students enough opportunity to process the reading materials effectively. The extended time helps the student to interpret the content effectively. They can look back, correct those misunderstandings and mistakes, seek explanations, and reread the text for a more extended period.

Strategies for Explosive Child Treatment at School

Explosive Disorder and School

Every child, regardless of gender, color, religious beliefs, or disability, has the right to a good education. An explosive child s is no different than any other child when it comes to understanding things around him or her. Getting diagnosed does not mean a child has a low IQ. There are many people with a high intelligence quotient who have explosive disorders. Any parent wants their child to have the best education possible, probably more so for parents of children who have special needs. The first thing to consider is finding the right school that will suit the child's learning style. Here are some suggestions about choosing a school for your child.

- **Know your child.** Look deeper into his/her behavior; observe how he or she learns and how he or she is as a student. Does he or she learn better by touch or by listening? Is he or she the type that does well in a group or alone? Does he or she like to volunteer, or do you need to draw him/her out? You should also consider his/her specific needs, such as a seat far from the window (for fewer distractions) or a teacher who can give him/her step-by-step instructions.

- **Check out, possible candidates.** Don't limit your research by just reading leaflets describing their services and academic accomplishments; get in-depth by interviewing teachers, guidance counselors, principals, and other special-needs providers. It is also essential to interview parents whose children are enrolled in the school to better view how the school works.

What Type of Students Will My Child Be Grouped With?

Of course, finding the right school is not the only thing you need to do to make sure your child is also getting the education he or she deserves. Cooperation with your child's teacher is also very important. Try to strengthen your child's relationship with his or her teacher at the start of the school year. Set a meeting face-to-face with the teacher to talk about your child. Be honest about your expectations and worries, as well as provide tips that might be able to help the teacher handle your child when he or she becomes disruptive. It's also a good idea to discuss what works best for your child in terms of learning styles. You can also set up regular contact with the teacher, such as weekly progress reports, daily phone calls, or emails.

It is also a good idea to ask about helpful classroom accommodations for your child, such as:

- A seating arrangement closer to the teaching area and farther away from possible distractions, such as a window or door.
- Reduced workload (both in homework and schoolwork) to take into account the child's attention span.

- Allowing extra time for the child to finish tests and assignments and providing a quiet space for him/her to take these tests to avoid distractions.

Defiant Children and Nonverbal Communication

Why is it so important to understand the value of nonverbal communication in teaching and learning? In moments of high social pressure from peers, nonverbal communication will always be one of the most, if not the most, essential skills to possess. Social pressure brings about the times when humans will think the most thoughts in their heads, while also acting the least on those ideas. Where is social pressure always present? It is an educational atmosphere filled with teaching and learning. We'll discuss teaching and learning in the school setting primarily.

A teacher's inner dialogue commonly includes; what is the level of respect my students exhibit towards me? Are they listening and paying attention to my words? How can I be cool and relatable without crossing the line and becoming a pushover? Am I an effective teacher with helpful lessons? The list goes on forever.

Relating to Teachers

If you have a good working relationship with your instructor, you will encourage your child's progress at school. Yet partnerships can be compromised if you consider that his instructor is incompetent or if, conversely, his teacher thinks you are not doing an excellent parenting job. That can happen if there is no contact with you. So how do you develop a relationship with the teacher of your child?

Daily Reports

Term report cards for many years have been with us. Nevertheless, it is now customary to use daily reports to track children living with explosive synths. Regular updates have been widely accepted as they have some apparent advantages. Knowing what happened during your child's school day can be very helpful. Such data helps you to deal with problems efficiently and avoid them before they get worse.

Daily coverage can be troublesome as educators often pull parents into issues that can be easily handled throughout the day of class. As school issues leak into the evening hours, most parents are upset. Instead, such problems monopolize family time, and parents are fearful of every report.

You can also be pushed into an official by the monitoring system. The child is likely to interpret school events in terms that put him in a favorable light, although his instructor is likely to point out that something entirely different has happened. Under these conditions, you might place a strain on your relationship with him if you criticize your child when you haven't seen what happened. On the other hand, if you are side by side with your child, you risk undermining his teacher's credibility. Sadly, if you take a stand against his instructor, you might encourage future non-cooperative activities. Your child may get the message that his teacher's conduct was inappropriate, and he may wonder if listening to her makes sense at all. In particular, if your child has often felt chastised at home, he might like the fact that you are now fighting for him instead of criticizing him. In class, he will continue to create drama because he loves your encouragement. As you can see, teacher upheaval poses the same kinds of issues as in family triangles.

Know the favorite activities of the rest of the students. If the whole classroom loves a certain privilege, then so will the defiant child due to the effect of herd behavior. No one enjoys being left out while they watch their peers have fun. If the child does not comply after the second command, you follow through with your threats, ignore them and focus on those who are doing great.

Nothing provides comfort to children like familiar surroundings, and their behavior is not as harshly judged by those who understand what they are going through.

When it comes to an explosive child, teachers, and parents are advised to use one of two strategies. These rules guide the dos and don'ts to make the child's school life easier.

In such an instance, if the teacher understood the child's needs and had provided the three questions instead, then the assignment would be submitted as complete, with enough effort placed in it. By avoiding long assignments, the child's first thought is not to just complete the assignment, so it is out of the way—but they put effort into it as well and in this way, they don't fail in class.

Consider a child who has difficulty organizing their work. They are constantly misplacing and forgetting their homework or which assignments must be completed first. It becomes chaotic and stressful for them, especially when the teacher is unsure how to assist.

The teacher may believe that things are not going well at home, which is stressing the child, and that calling the parent is not a good idea. They only have one other option, which is to assemble a person in a better position to study the child and advise on the best course of action to be taken. Then, once they are certain of what is going on, they involve the parent.

While parents often want to be the first to be notified, it should not bother them that the teacher sought outside help first because then this shows that they are just as invested in the child.

Punishments are learning experiences. They are not intended to cause the child pain, but rather to teach him or her. Punishing a child with disorder explosions with something that helps them gain control is not recommended. This would be physical exercise; punishing them by not allowing them to participate in sports, which would provide them with an outlet, would exacerbate their aggression and resentment.

Don't Use Negative Words

It is essential to insist on positivity while playing with a child with explosive attacks. It would work if you gave feedback but positively provide them so that your child's confidence level increases. If you keep making them, feel that whatever they do is wrong, they will start feeling that no one loves them. That makes the outbursts worse and sometimes even out of control. The use of any form of harmful language is wrong for an explosive kid or all children.

Discipline for the Classroom

Defiant children enjoy pushing your buttons and finding out how much compliance they can get out of you! Yes, children naturally know how to get compliance out of adults. Heck, kids understand better than adults the best ways to achieve goals. Coming from infancy as babies who had to use nonverbal communication to get food, they depended on other people's willingness to comply with their requests. They used smiling, laughing, crying, pointing, and outright determination. On the other hand, adults become so prideful in their independence that they forget what it takes to get the most out of other people. It is important to understand when and how to discipline an oppositional defiant child. For example, a common defiant behavior is a child who tells authority figures "no" when it is time to put games away or complete classwork. You can simply ignore the child and give extra treats to those students who are listening. The defiant child wants you to beg them to complete their work. They want everyone in the class to look at them while you argue and try to sort out a solution. This is where a defiant child will try to embarrass your authority power. What is your resolution to this scenario? Give your command once (e.g., Get in line please). If they say no, try putting a consequence behind the command while still maintaining a calm voice (e.g., Get in line or you won't watch the movie later, get in line or go to the office). Here, you see that the consequence should be taking away a privilege that they love or one that involves the child having to deal with a higher authority figure (e.g., the principal or other high-power disciplinary figure in the school). Look the child directly in their eyes and ignore them if they fail to listen after the second time. It works in your favor and gains respect from the child because they know that you are not going to overreact to their defiance.

Strategies for Behavioral Disorder Treatment at School

Teachers frequently have a more difficult time dealing with children and cannot do it all on their own. As previously stated, when a parent drops their child off and calls it a day, they do not transfer responsibility to the teacher. There is significantly more at stake than simply attending PTA meetings at the school, and they must collaborate to help the child. There are, however, things both the parent and teacher can do to help the kid at school.

This responsibility doesn't always fall on just the two. The school, as an institution, also plays a role in this. They have a responsibility to educate their staff and other students about mental health issues. The school may decide to provide special education learning, not to separate the children by dividing them into different classes but to provide the children with an opportunity to learn and be among other people understand them.

Behavioral Management

This is just as the name suggests. Its focus is on the behavior of the child and how their emotions affect them. How teachers and parents handle a situation without undermining the child's self-esteem. Teachers understand how to help the child on a personal level, as well as the child's emotions and approach to situations. To avoid the development of negative behavior, this strategy entails encouraging positive behavior and rewarding it. All this without making the child feel like they are receiving preferential treatment.

Organization Management

One of the biggest challenges that explosive children encounter in school is the ability to stay organized. Their explosions frequently produce sloppy work, and their lack of organization skills, as a result, disadvantages them in class performance. Helping the children with this goes a long way toward helping the child achieve better results, which in turn boosts their self-esteem.

Tips for Teachers

Provide Clear Assignment Instructions

When the teacher gives instructions, the child is frequently absent-minded and daydreaming, and he or she misses what is said. When the teacher realizes this about the child and that their behavior is not intentional, they devise strategies to ensure that the same information shared with the other children is not missed by the explosive child. How will they go about it? Questioning the student to see if they understand. They could also call the student after class and go over the assignment with them to ensure the student understands what is expected of them. In this case, it is also critical to check in on the student's assignment progress regularly.

Pay Attention to Behavior

Most teachers who work with teenagers and children are already familiar with and have experience with how children behave. They understand that passive aggression is very common in children and, as a result, they frequently ignore it. Teachers must become more aware of mental health issues and learn to recognize warning signs when behavior deviates from the norm. When a child is extremely agitated and continues to pick fights with everyone or speak back to the teacher to avoid being sent out of the classroom. Of course, is not an excuse for bad behavior, and such behavior should not be rewarded by not punishing it; however, there is a source for that behavior, and punishing the child without addressing the source of the problem does not accomplish much.

Sensitize Themselves on Explosive Disorder Influence on Emotions

Teachers' reactions to explosive students can make or break them. Children who are unable to focus long enough to complete their tasks are sensitive to criticism. At this point, the children believe what adults in positions of authority tell them. It is very easy to break a child's spirit by verbally attacking them when they are unable to complete a project instead of helping them get past it.

Teachers must understand why those children behave the way they do. Always engaging in risky activities, he is sometimes referred to as the "class clown" by his peers.

Avoid Long and Repetitive Assignments

This is related to the attention span issue. Long assignments easily bore and distract explosive children. Returning to the previous example of a child skipping five questions because they know that if they put effort into the work, they will only manage three and mark the assignment as incomplete. However, if you just do all five with no effort, the assignment is complete, even if it is done poorly.

Allow Breaks

Teachers need to encourage movement and exercise. A one-and-a-half-hour class is taxing on any child, not just those with the disorder. Half an hour has passed, and the child is already bored out of their minds, their attention diverted elsewhere. To make the class more engaging, a teacher can devise a plan to involve the students. Maintain your conversation with them. Incorporate stories into the lesson, or even have them stand for a few minutes. Explosive children have a very short attention span and find it difficult to concentrate, so making classwork something they enjoy and look forward to can help.

Apply Organization Tools

This covers the use of files, directories, and lists, among other things. This is meant to help children keep track of the things they need to do and trace their activities. An explosive child already struggles with organizational skills and is easily distracted. Keeping a file with their homework allows the child and parent to track progress and serves as a reminder for the child when they forget to do something. They can always return to the folder or list to see what is expected of them.

Minimize Distractions

Children can be easily distracted by the smallest things. During class, the teacher should discourage interruptions to ensure the children focus on the lesson. Teachers would always aim to have their students learn something at the end of the day. This is impossible to achieve if there are constant distractions. While children who do not have any disorder can recover from a distraction and return their attention to their teacher, those who do have explosive disorder find it difficult to concentrate once the focus has been lost.

Communicate With Parents

Before making any other decisions, such as consulting a counselor, communication between the parent and the instructor should be the first step. The first thing that a teacher should do when they notice that a child's behavior is not typical is to contact the parent. The parents understand their child best—the teacher can have conversations with them, and exchange notes to see if the child's behavior is exclusive to school grounds or if it happens everywhere.

Involve School Guidance and Counselor

In most cases, this follows after contacting the parent. However, a teacher may be suspicious of a child's behavior but be unsure whether their suspicions are correct or not. Guidance counselors at school are more than just teachers. Teachers are not expected to know everything, so having someone point out things they do not understand helps.

Create Clear Rules

Teachers need to create rules and state the consequences when children fail to follow them. As stated earlier, while explosive disorder is a mental disorder that limits a child's executive functions, children with this condition are still children. The condition should not be used to excuse bad behavior. When they break the rules, they should receive punishment for their actions and reward when they do good.

Try to Make Learning Fun

Very few children enjoy learning, and they will all give you different reasons why it is not fun for them. Engaging children in studies has proven to be a beneficial method, and the children who require this type of learning the most are those with explosive disorders.

Those children respond better to things that interest them—when an assignment is made to be a game, they will want to play. This is like what parents do at home to make sure their child is engaged in the work they are doing. Using apples to help with their math problems, using other fruits to help with identifying color, or silly acronyms, and letting the creative side of the child influence their studies.

Chapter 13. ADHD Skills and Development

Have you or anybody you know been diagnosed with attention deficit hyperactivity disorder (ADHD)? There are 12 important skills you should know about and assist them in developing, whether it's a child or an adult.

Here are some insights into these skills as well as tips for development:

1. **Time management and organization.** This includes being able to plan, schedule events, and execute tasks in accordance with the time frame set, dividing long-term projects into short-term goals, and prioritizing tasks. The tips are obvious—help them stay organized and be goal-oriented.

2. **They need to learn how to prioritize tasks and tasks that aren't as important.** This is a good daily life skill that adults, as well as children with ADHD, may have trouble mastering.

3. **Learning from mistakes or errors.** We all make mistakes but for those with ADHD, this can be an especially challenging skill to develop. They really do need your help in realizing the importance of creating new plans based on what went wrong with the old one and using this information to improve the plan or task at hand. They also need your patience; so, don't get upset or angry when they try again and fail again because they will fail before they succeed. Remember they are learning, so be encouraging and supportive.

4. **Properly organizing them.** One of the most serious issues that people with ADHD experience is not knowing how or when to stop or postpone when it comes to getting things done. Make sure they understand how important organization is to accomplish tasks and projects on time.

5. **Being able to focus for long periods.** This is usually a skill that you can develop in childhood but can become a bigger problem as you get older if not worked on consistently throughout your life. Many adults with ADHD can focus extremely well on things that they are interested in but have a hard time paying attention to things they aren't interested in.

6. **Staying on task and finishing what is started.** For many of those with ADHD, it's very easy to get distracted by something else or change their minds midway through a project. This may lead to the tasks not being done at all or having to be redone. If you know someone who has this problem, help them learn how to stay committed and focused on a task until it is finished.

7. **Noticing details that others miss**. This characteristic of those with ADD/ADHD can be a blessing as well as a curse. For example, an adult with this skill can point out typos or grammatical errors in a paper, which may help you not to look bad when you hand it in. It can also cause problems such as hyper-focus on something that may not be important, like a small stain on the wall. If they are aware that they tend to notice things others don't, and if they have the proper support and training so that it doesn't become a distraction, this is a skill that can be developed and used positively.

8. **Being able to multi-task.** Just because someone has ADHD doesn't mean that he or she can't learn how to do something else while doing another thing at the same time. For example, a teenager might learn how to do his math homework while listening to his iPod. This is a skill that all people need to develop and build upon.

9. **Learning from others' mistakes and experiences.** This can be difficult, especially if they don't take much time to learn from them. For example, you tell someone with ADHD that he can't go out with friends because he didn't finish his chores or didn't get his homework done, but he still goes out even though you told him not to. This is

where the problem lies – just because you've told them once doesn't mean that they'll remember what you said next time.

10. **Being in control of their own actions and behavior.** This is the first "big" issue that they need to learn. If they don't know how to guide their own behavior, they will continue to engage in dangerous or risky behaviors and could get into trouble.

11. **Working with others, as well as working independently.** This may seem very simple, but it's something many adults struggle within a daily basis. They have difficulty understanding what's expected of them and can drift off-topic or lose focus when speaking. It's also difficult for them to ask for help in getting a task done because they may not realize it is needed or that the task is demanding enough for others to help them out too much.

12. **Being able to accept responsibility for their actions and thoughts.** This is a very difficult concept for those with ADD/ADHD to grasp. They tend to blame others for their mistakes, get frustrated easily, and can be hypersensitive to what's going on around them. With this in mind, you should make sure that they understand how important it is to take responsibility for any and all actions that they commit as well as how important it is to learn from their mistakes.

As you can see, ADHD affects not only those who have the disorder but also family members and friends. Everyone in the family should work together to acquire these talents so that everyone succeeds in life.

Chapter 14. Medication and Treatment, Different Type of Therapies

Many medical professionals agree that developing consistent and effective behavior management techniques is essential for managing an ADD/ADHD disorder when raising children. Applying behavioral strategies is necessary for parenting in the home, modifying or managing behavior in the classroom, or particular education placement. Behavioral management strategies can be helpful for infants of all ages, sorting from kids younger than five up to 18. The modeling principles here are the same as with any child: immediately reinforce positive behavior with reward or praise and curb bad behavior by allowing consequences to develop naturally.

When it comes to five or younger children that may be displaying beginning symptoms of ADD/ADHD, it's imperative to provide a structured and routine environment throughout the week. Be sure to let the child know beforehand if something in the usual routine will change. It helps young children to have expectations, boundaries and develop trust at this age. Making a habit of giving these children instructions and preparing them beforehand makes complex and straightforward tasks easier to accomplish.

As your child grows to ages 6–9 years, creating a precise and predictable reward or merit system is an effective way to model positive behavior. Make it centered on time doing a favorite activity instead of providing candy or snacks. Instead, provide the child with a steady diet of learning activities like reading and puzzles. Be sure to participate in the young child's activities since they learn the most from you. Several parents find it helpful to use a timer to provide more structure to their schedules. Setting time limits beforehand will help the child expect time limits on fun and tedious activities. This method is beneficial when the child receives a reward at the end of the predetermined time limit. It also gives them a deadline or ending for how long they have to focus on one thing before going on to another.

Older children up to age 12 still need clear instructions daily. A predetermined reward system also works well for this age group. It's essential to have a predetermined or private approach to disciplining negative behavior to avoid the embarrassment that a sensitive child with ADD/ADHD may experience. Keep an open communication line with the child's teachers to identify and address behavior problems before any classroom situations get out of control. This preemptive approach will also help mitigate the teachers' likelihood of getting frustrated with the child's ADD/ADHD disorder.

In addition to looking at how ADD/ADHD can be managed at different ages, there are common behavioral issues that many parents struggle with. Here are some ideas and strategies to implement at home with your child.

- **Managing impulsivity.** Children with ADD/ADHD are very impulsive and do not always think before acting. While it may seem like they are purposely defying you, they have difficulty controlling their impulses in reality. To help teach your child to think before they act, tell them to stop and think if they are about to do something they know is wrong. Teach them to count to themselves, to five or ten, depending on their age, while taking deep breaths. It brings oxygen into the brain and will help them think clearly. Then have them ask themselves, what will happen if I do this? Repeat this process with your child. You teach them to control their impulsivity, regain control of their body and mind through deep breathing, and help them understand the consequences of their actions.
- **High energy levels.** Children with ADD/ADHD typically have higher energy levels than other children. It can sometimes get them

into trouble, especially if they are bored. If they're bored, they'll find something to do, whether or not it's acceptable. The key to curbing behavior is to keep your child busy and active. Sign them up for sports, take them on outings to the park, or play catch with them in the backyard. Children with ADD/ADHD need this positive outlet for all of their energy. Try to find other fun activities in your community that you can participate in. Many places offer fun activities for children and families if you do a little research. By continually keeping your child busy with festive activities, you will reduce the boredom and tendency to find activities on their own.

- **Forgetfulness.** While all children need reminders to bring their lunch to school or comb their hair, children with ADD/ADHD will need more. They may have the good intention of going upstairs to get their jacket, only to be distracted by the toys in their room. Understand that they are not trying to aggravate you but need gentle reminders. If you've sent your child up for their jacket, and they are taking too long, you can say, "Jacket," up the stairs to help them get back on track. Visuals may also work well with assisting them to remember. If they always have to bring certain things to school, you could create a visual that they place by their backpack. Every day before they leave, they have to check that visual. Now, you may have to remind them to prevent it, but then part of the responsibility goes back to them.

- **Focus and concentration.** While each child with ADD/ADHD will struggle with this, you can provide an environment that can help them as a parent. Take the time, to observe when your child is most alert during the day and at which times they may struggle. Perhaps some specific triggers or transitions cause your child to be very distracted. For example, it could be when they first arrive home from school, or when you go somewhere out of the ordinary that's not in the routine. Once you are aware of these times or triggers, work around them, so

136

your child is doing their schoolwork at times when they are at their best. It is also good to create an accessible working environment from other distractions, such as toys, TV, or video games. Working together with your child on homework or schoolwork will also help keep them on track. Allowing your child to be active and move around the room will also aid concentration or learning. For example, if your child is a wiggler, try having them sit on an exercise ball while doing their work. They can continuously be rocking and moving while working.

These are just a few ideas to try when working with a child with ADD/ADHD. Try to individualize these approaches, depending on your child's needs and what seems to work for your family. If you need help improving your child's behavioral management tactics with ADHD, don't be afraid to seek expert advice. Many specialists will come into the home and work with the family on behavior management strategies. Over time, as you implement these strategies, you can begin to see positive changes in your child's behavior.

Cognitive Behavior Therapy

The psychologist uses this strategy to get a child to speak their way about what is going on around them and then be more reasoned and analytical about their reactions. The hope is that the cognitively educated infant will finally learn to calm down and self-regulate their actions. It seems to be a suitable care choice for any child with ADHD, but the findings have been frustrating.

Young ADHD kids are too impulsive to think anything out before responding, and older kids aren't different. The approach is helpful in the silent, disorganized, inattentive form of ADHD. It has a role in treating children and adults with ADHD, but only after stimulant therapy has been used to help them concentrate.

Education in social skills ADHD children tend to be oblivious to how their acts offend others.

They are severely disadvantaged due to their lack of social awareness, and when the methodology of social skills training became accessible, we saw it as a revolutionary development. Children learn how their actions and attitudes influence those around them in this class. While they communicate well, their positive behavior is reinforced; when they interact poorly, they were expected to consider how their actions affect others.

While social skills training seem necessary for all children with ADHD, the findings have been mixed. According to research, relational skills should be learned in the therapy room, but the benefits have little use outside of the therapy room.

Integration of the senses Jean Ayres, an American therapist, popularized sensory integration in the early 1970s. Her primary emphasis was on the intellectual disorders often associated with ADHD. Movement, swinging, turning, and balancing are among her strategies. These acts are believed to aid brain growth and have consequences for academic and other skills. Kinesiologists also use related techniques. Although a few Australian centers now advocate for Ayres' work, we do not prescribe these ideas to our patients. According to recent research findings, sensory integration has no psychological benefit over more conventional approaches.

Occupational therapy is a form of therapy that focuses on most ADHD children who have poor handwriting. A successful occupational therapist can assist with this by working on the pen grasp, letter organization, and word movement. Occupational therapy and stimulant medicine are commonly used to assist with neatness and precision.

Many ADHD kids struggle with motor planning and balance, making it difficult to tie their shoes, pitch a straight ball, catch a ball, or walk quickly. A quick session with an optimistic therapist will assist a kid in getting the most of what they have while also improving self-confidence. Occupational therapy can help a kid with two left feet develop in specific ways, but it can never transform into a world-class athlete or elegant dancer.

The Talking Cures

The majority of private child psychologists in Australia in the early 1980s were more interested in the environmental-analytical approach than the biological–behavioral approach. All of my colleagues in Sydney and Melbourne concluded that ADHD habits were caused by unresolved emotions, dysfunctions, and past experiences in the parents' lives. Parents were often referred to long-term counseling to discuss their potential issues, although confident children were kept occupied through play.

These theories were 20 years behind North America's pragmatic, eclectic viewpoints. Any medical practitioner, such as the late Dr. Gordon Serfontein, opposed these ingrained Australian views, seeing ADHD as a hereditary, biological condition not exacerbated by bad parenting. In the mid-1980s, Serfontein and others were accused of conspiring with parents to save them from owning up to their part in developing the disease. There was even more uproar when these "parental issues" were handled with stimulant drugs.

While some prominent "mind therapists" are dissatisfied with our views— those parents are not to blame and ADHD is the product of a brain dysfunction—they are now a "shrinking minority." Most child psychiatrists and counselors now believe that play therapy for an inattentive, unthinking child is ineffective. The so-called "talking cures" have a role in handling confident parents' emotional difficulties but not treating ADHD. Formal family therapy is largely ineffective, but intelligent psychiatrists use a less traditional approach to help all family members accept their ADHD sibling.

Psychiatrists now play an essential part in diagnosing, developing behavioral programs, helping caregivers, and administering medicine.

Eye drills for children with developmental optometry: Many regular adults and children will slightly vary as to their vision, and eye motions were checked in depth. Many people specializing in testing development believe that these minor issues with eye control are related to learning disabilities.

Any of the ADHD kids in our treatment who are poor readers have been diagnosed. Any ADHD children under our care who are bad learners have been sent to developmental optometrists by their schools. Parents often come to our office upset that our hospital vision doctors refused to identify a serious problem. Many of these children were given eye exercises or low-powered lenses. Few people, in our experience, stay with these for longer than a few months.

Policy announcements on vision and learning have been released by the American Academy of Pediatrics and the Australian College of Pediatrics. In essence, they conclude that such therapies are of little too little use to most children.

Tinted Lenses

Helen Irlen, a Californian, copyrighted such lens tints in the mid-1980s, claiming that they benefited the reading impaired. The media reacted positively, with stories on "60 Minutes" and significant publications. Few trials seem to have shown the initial claims of success. The essential findings show that a small subset of people could benefit, but the data is mostly unimpressive.

140

Zinc and Multivitamins

Vitamin B6 was said to help both inattentive and learning-disabled children in the early 1980s. Then there was the claim that zinc could help with ADHD and autism. Multivitamins are now very widespread. According to credible reports, there is no evidence that any of these remedies positively impacts ADHD or its related learning disorders. Extra vitamins can help with poor absorption and famine relief, but they can't help with learning and behavior.

Natural Medicines

Natural treatments and plant extracts have sparked a lot of concern in treating ADHD. We don't have tunnel vision or demand that physicians prescribe drugs; we ask for fairness. Before being approved for sale, years of growth, double-blind trials, and meticulous testing went into Ritalin. This license has been thoroughly researched in the 45 years since it was issued. A natural substance is not subject to the same prohibitions. Many enter the market with no credible proof of effectiveness and little assurance of long-term protection. We don't object to natural therapies; we object to unjust arguments that a comparatively unproven natural substance is as successful as and safer than a thoroughly researched medication.

Natural treatments are well-known for having a slew of adverse side effects. Naturalness does not imply safety—opium, snake poison, and nicotine are all very crude. Stimulants are successful in over 80% of children with ADHD, according to over 150 double-blind, controlled trials. For statistics like this, it's plain to see why parents search out untested and unproven treatments.

Entrapment of neurons—biofeedback—sugar. We also see children who have received cranial stimulation and neck realignment from alternative practitioners. The parents claim that their child's blood supply to the base of the brain was obstructed or that a nerve was entrapped inside the skull. These arguments are, without a doubt, false, according to our expert neurologists. Our sports stars must be losing a lot of understanding every week if subtle touch to the neck and skull will realign areas of the brain. One of the approaches being marketed is biofeedback. The infant stares at a computer screen that displays an image related to tracing their brainwave function. They improve the drawing by changing their thinking; with the theory, you will refrain from feedback. Many medications are needed to be safe, and they are not inexpensive. We know that the most powerful of our American colleagues are against this kind of therapy.

Sugar is once again under attack. It's probably a product of our puritan upbringing, which told us that something that causes us satisfaction is perhaps wrong. Parents often say that substituting honey for sugar results in improved actions, but this has been extensively investigated and shown to be entirely incorrect. Honey is honey that has been recycled by a bee and has a variety of preservatives and contaminants from nature. Sugar, without a doubt, rots children's teeth and makes them obese, but studies have proven that it has little impact on learning or behavior.

Multi-Modal Treatment

We know that three types of treatment can help ADHD patients: medication, behavior modification, and a combination of the two. Multi-modal treatment for ADHD patients entails using various strategies and techniques to manage the disease's symptoms.

Using a variety of treatments on children improves their chances of overcoming the condition. Many types of behavioral therapy do not require medication, and I will go over each detail to understand the service and its effects. You can suggest these behavior modification treatments to your doctor, who will be able to tell you which ones are best for your child. Many psychiatrists have used and researched all of these treatments in the past.

Behavioral Modification

For the past three decades, therapists have used Behavior Modification treatments to manage ADHD. Because of their experience and ability to cure many children of aggressive and disruptive behavior, these techniques have gained a lot of respect over the years. With the assistance of these methods, children with ADHD have learned to manage their actions, develop positive social skills, and improve their academic performance. There are five types of behavior modification treatments for children with ADHD:

- Cognitive behavioral interventions
- Clinical behavior therapy
- Direct contingency management
- Intensive behavioral treatments
- Behavioral and pharmacological treatment combination

Cognitive Behavior Therapy

This type of treatment, often abbreviated to CBT, is ideal for parents who want to be involved and active in their child's clinical development. CBT aims to teach parents and other caregivers how to manage their children's ADHD symptoms. CBT typically consists of training programs or individual sessions in which a therapist discusses how you can modify your child's behavior.

One of the characteristics of having an ADHD child is that it causes many doubts, irrational thoughts, and unrealistic expectations. While other therapies focus on direct actions, CBT assists you in removing the barriers that prevent you from assisting your child in overcoming his ADHD symptoms.

When it comes to ADHD and their child, many of the parents I speak with admitting to the following habits when assessing their child's development:

- **Exaggeration**—these parents believe that a single negative aspect of ADHD is more significant than all others. As a result, they may overlook significant broader progress.
- **It's all or nothing**—if it doesn't work correctly, it doesn't work at all! Parents must recognize that each milestone achieved is perfect in its own right. When it comes to ADHD treatment, there is no such thing as "all or nothing." Patience pays off.
- **"Should" thinking**—this type of thought process causes self-resentment when you fail to do something you believe you should do. However, there are no "should." Just keep doing what the professional has asked or advised you to do, and don't add to your stress by constantly researching what else you could do to help your child.
- **Comparative thinking**—this can be harmful to the mind. When you negatively compare yourself to other parents of ADHD children, remember that each ADHD case is unique.
- **Personalization**—you are emotionally invested in your child's illness. You can ask yourself, "What did I do to deserve this?" or you can decide, "This is karma at work." It's not your fault that you have a difficult life or that your child has ADHD (unless you did not take care of yourself during pregnancy). As a result, don't take things personally.

Once you recognize such thoughts as disabling, you can confidently eliminate them and focus on the actual plan with the help of CBT. You must understand that you must first change your thoughts to make a significant difference in your child's life and mind.

Cognitive Behavioral Interventions

This method is commonly referred to as CBI. The goal of CBI is to focus on self-control through verbal self-instruction and problem-solving strategies, self-monitoring and evaluation, cognitive modeling, and other similar techniques. Your child will meet with a therapist once or twice a week to learn these strategies through methods such as role-play.

Therapists use a popular CBI technique that teaches a child to "stop" when disruptive. Introducing these self-instruction techniques is that children with ADHD do not have the motivation to give themselves cues on what to do. Cognitive Behavioral Interventions are becoming less popular as ADHD experts focus on developing alternative techniques.

Contingency Management

This type of behavioral treatment, known as CM, follows a structured format and may include a special treatment classroom. The encouragement of actions through positive or negative reinforcement is one of the main principles used in CM. It entails using economic tokens as behavioral tools, such as giving or withholding rewards. Though most parents use reward systems with their children, knowing the most effective methods of achieving results can be beneficial. After receiving CM treatment, your child will be better able to respond to your cues as well as the prohibitions and privileges you grant him.

Intensive Behavioral Treatments

It entails children, parents, and teachers implementing techniques that reward children for good behavior. The combination of methods aims to improve socialization, self-control, and academic abilities. Your child will attend school and perform better willingly by the end of Intensive Behavioral Treatment.

Several Intensive Behavioral Treatment Summer Camps are available, each lasting about eight weeks and perfectly timed before the school year. The typical mix of behavioral treatment and recreational activities at these camps ensures that the therapy is beneficial and enjoyable for the children.

Combination of Pharmacological and Behavioral Interventions

Many ADHD children have benefited from a combination of medication and behavioral treatment in the past. It outperforms either behavioral or drug treatment alone. When both medication and behavioral therapy are used, therapists will usually reduce the doses and medicines used during behavioral sessions. However, keep in mind that the individual patient will always determine the best use and combination of treatments.

Effects of Medication on Children With ADHD

The impact of ADHD medication on motor activity and coordination is a significant side effect to consider. You may notice that your child's activity level in school has decreased due to medication treatment. It means he isn't running around as much as he used to. Additionally, you will notice an improvement in the neatness of your child's handwriting. We will see similar enhancements in other arts and crafts activities. Your children will be able to play with clay, building blocks, and other constructive toys much more effectively.

In terms of cognitive effects, you will notice that your child has a longer attention span. He won't be as easily distracted in the future. He will be able to concentrate better on instructions. He will also experience a decrease in impulsivity and an increase in productivity. When asked to do something, he is likely to do it carefully and thoroughly. You will notice a significant improvement in accuracy and speed of work. When you consider how much medication allows new information to enter your child's brain, you can see how beneficial meditation can be.

And the most significant effect of any medication is its influence on social behavior. Being able to interact more effectively with others is critical in dealing with ADHD. Children on ADHD medication no longer seek attention in the classroom from other children or educators because their inattentive, off-task behaviors are reduced. When they interact with other people, they show less anger and more self-control. Their social skills can improve so dramatically that you can safely include your child in organized sports like basketball or soccer. Aggression and oppositional behavior are reduced, bossiness is eliminated, and children begin to consider other people's perspectives.

Interpersonal refers to relationships with others and their social abilities, i.e., how they usually relate to and interact with others. Many people seek therapy to address relationship issues, such as a separation or resolving a conflict with a loved one. Others seek treatment because they have become isolated or detached.

The seventh modality comprises medications, health and wellness, and biology. This method includes a variety of aspects, such as physical health and wellness (e.g., illness, health and wellness conditions, physical limitations, age-related health and wellness issues, chronic discomfort), organic factors (e.g., mind chemistry or genetics), and the requirement for drug or other types of clinical/organic therapy. This modality also includes a way of life routines that influence one's health, such as exercise (or lack thereof), diet regimen and nourishment, rest habits, alcohol, overindulging, medication use, cigarette smoking routines, and so on.

The specialist in multi-modal therapy analyzes these seven modalities in two (2) ways: by speaking with the client and having him or filling out a questionnaire known as the Multimodal Life History Inventory.

Chapter 15. Prioritizing a Healthy Diet: What to Eat and What to Avoid

They are the foods and supplements you take. Your daily diet plans should help your brain function well and reduce symptoms, such as restlessness or inability to sustain concentration.

You could focus on these choices:

- **Overall nutrition.** The assumption is that the foods you eat will make your symptoms better or worse. You might not be eating some foods that might help you get better.
- **Supplements.** With this, you add nutritional supplements, nutrients, and vitamins to your diet. The theory is that it could help you make up for the inadequate nutrient. It is believed that if you don't get enough nourishment, it could worsen your symptoms
- **Remove diets.** This involves not eating foods or things that trigger your symptoms or worsen them.

Top Foods for the Explosive Disorder

- **Additive-free and unprocessed foods.** Due to the harmful nature of additives, you should eat fresh and unprocessed foods. Additives include artificial sweeteners, preservatives, and colorings which can be found in processed foods, they are detrimental to explosive children.
- **Chicken.** Tryptophan is an important amino acid that aids in the body's protein synthesis and serotonin production. Serotonin

induces sleep, happy emotions, and helps with impulse control and hostility.

- **Eat breakfast.** For most children with explosive disorders, breakfast helps the body regulate bloodstream sugars and stabilize hormonal fluctuations. Eat breakfast that has at least 20 grams of proteins. Try my Thin Mint Proteins Smoothie which has 20 grams of proteins; it is a delicious and filling way to "break the fast."
- **Wild-caught salmon.** It is not only rich in vitamin B-6 but is also filled with omega 3. According to the institution of Maryland hospital, a scientific trial indicated that lower examples of omega-3 EFA's solved learning and behavioral problems (like those related to disorder explosions) than kids with reasonable levels of omega. Individuals, including children, should eat healthy salmons at least twice a week.

Foods to Avoid

- **Sugar.** This is the main trigger for children. Avoid any type of refined sugar including chocolate, desserts, soda, or fruit drinks.
- **Gluten.** Some researchers and parents observe worsening behavior when a child eats gluten, which can indicate sensitivity to the protein in wheat. Avoid all foods made with whole wheat grains such as bread, pasta, and whole wheat grains cereal. Seek out gluten-free and even grain-free alternatives.
- **Milk products.** Most cow milk contains A1 which may trigger the same reaction as gluten and, so should be avoided. If severe symptoms occur after eating milk products, discontinue use. Goat's milk doesn't include proteins and it is a better option for explosive children.
- **Food color and dyes.** Children could be allergic to food dyes and colorings; therefore, all processed foods should be avoided.

Colorings and dyes can be found in nearly every commercially prepared food. Food dyes can be found in energy drinks, chocolates, wedding cakes mix, chewable nutritional supplements as well as toothpaste!

- **Caffeine.** Even though some studies prove that caffeine might help with some behavioral disorder symptoms, it pays to lessen or avoid caffeine; however, even these studies haven't been validated. The side-effect of caffeine, include anxiousness, and nervousness. All these can further worsen the explosive symptoms.

- **MSG and HVP.** These additives are believed to lessen dopamine amounts in children and adults. Dopamine is from the brain's pleasure and prize systems. For children battling with behavioral disorder explosions, well-balanced dopamine is essential.

- **Nitrites.** Commonly found in lunch meat, canned foods, and several processed foods. Nitrites are connected with a child's growth, type one diabetes, certain types of malignancy, and IBS. It could result in an increased heartbeat, difficulty breathing, and restlessness that aggravate explosive disorder explosions symptoms.

- **Artificial sweeteners.** Artificial sweeteners are harmful to your health, and for dealing with the behavioral disorder; the unwanted effects could be damaging. Artificial sweeteners create biochemical adjustments in the body, which can affect cognitive function and psychological balance.

- **Allergens/things that trigger allergies.** Eliminate the top seven allergens, including soy, wheat, and milk, peanuts, tree nuts, eggs, and shellfish. Furthermore, eliminate any foods or drinks that are personal contaminants in the air. This may include papaya, avocados, bananas, kiwis (for people with latex allergies), coriander, caraway or fennel (all the same family), and chocolates.

Supplements for the Explosive Disorder

Some experts advise that explosive children take 100% vitamin and nutrient supplements each day. Other diet experts believe that individuals who take balanced meals don't need a supplement or micronutrient supplements. They claim there is no scientific evidence that vitamin or mineral supplements help all those with the disorder. While multivitamins would help for children, teens, and adults who don't balance their meals, several doses of vitamins could be toxic, avoid them.

Symptoms of explosive disorder differ from person to person. Work closely with a medical doctor, if you're taking supplements. To help yourself, you need to identify the food that is making your symptoms worse and endeavor to eliminate it from your diet. If the symptoms disappear, ensure you steer clear of the food and avoid it entirely.

If you cut out your favorite food from your daily diet, does your symptom worsen? Research is ongoing in this area, and the details aren't explicit.

Iron Supplementation

More studies are being conducted that show the effects low iron can have on children. When we think of a lack of iron, we think of those that are suffering from blood loss. When our bodies are lacking this basic mineral, a lot can happen, including an increase in our disorder explosions symptoms. It affects more than you might expect.

Iron is important to our bodies because it is what is responsible for making sure that oxygen makes its way to our vital organs and all of our muscles. We also need it for proper brain function. When we are lacking iron, it can also slow the production of dopamine, which is essential for those that want to live a happy, healthy life. If our explosive symptoms are out of control, then it might be a sign that we need more iron in our lives and diets.

Omega 3/6

Recent research has found that increasing our intake of healthy fat, such as that found in omega-rich meals, can aid in the normal generation of dopamine in our brains.

These fatty acids will improve brain function. While doing this, they will also increase attention. When brain function and attention increase, disorder explosions symptoms dramatically decrease. Along with more attention, these supplements can also help lessen restlessness, impulsivity, hyperactivity, and overall aggression in children. Some scientists even believe this is the best treatment for those that don't want to use any other medications.

Most researchers don't recommend this technique for controlling explosive disorder, however here are some common concerns and what professionals suggest: Food additives: In 1975, an allergist initially proposed that artificial colors, flavors, and preservatives might trigger hyperactivity in a few children. Child behavior experts have extensively argued this matter. Some said the thought of eliminating these ingredients from the diet is unfounded and unsupported by technology. However, one research demonstrates that food color and preservatives do increase hyperactivity in some children. However, the effects vary with age and type of additive.

Sugars: Some children become hyperactive after eating chocolate or other sugary foods. No study has proven that this triggers disorder explosions; however, sugary foods are best avoided.

Children that were given fish oil supplements were found to be better at reading and spelling, with overall improvements in their behavior as well. This means that kids can benefit greatly from including this supplement in their diet. In addition, it is one of the top natural depression fighters out there. As adults, we get even more health benefits from improving our omega-3 and 6 fatty acid consumption beyond just the reduction of our disorder explosions symptoms. These include an increase in eye health and a lower risk of heart disease developing.

To receive your FREE eBook "ADHD Organizing Solutions"

Scan this QR Code

Chapter 16. Mood Foods—Holistic Eating for Managing ADHD

Recent studies by Yunus (2019) from the renowned Exceptional Parent have asserted how there is a possible link between ADHD and high sugar, salt, and fat intake when kids receive diets with only minimal whole grains, fruits, and vegetable intakes (p. 24). Many findings specifically herald the benefits of a whole-food plant-based (WFPB) diet with minimal or no processing for protection against ADHD, cancers, heart disease, osteoporosis, and other chronic conditions (Yunus, 2019, p. 24) as well.

I am not suggesting a rigid "Biggest Loser" diet or any particular dietary model; I want to offer some natural foods and drinks to promote a better mood and mindful eating with tasty and healthier options for you and your kiddos. I also want to arm you with research and resources to explore and take it to the next level as far as what are best for your particular family's needs.

Are you ready for some yummy suggestions? Let us find those aprons, ok?

- **Snack Attacks:** Make snack attacks healthy with fresh fruits and veggies. Make nutritious smoothies together and add some chia and flax seeds to balance moods. MasterChef Junior, anyone?
- **Mr. and Ms. Clean:** This advice does not mean operating a pristine household free of dust bunnies and flawlessness, but it is about eating as clean as possible to avoid unnecessary additives and food colorings. Of course, kids are attracted to the colorful, marshmallow, vibrant products that are often so full of crap. Yunus (2019) also divulges how we have a clear responsibility as parents to purchase food products to ensure clean nutrition for children, tweens, and teens with ADHD.

"This is a controversial subject and, because we often have an emotional attachment to food, we are reluctant to look at this as an adjunct treatment" (p. 25).

- **Diggity D:** There is "No Diggity" about it that Vitamin D is the superior sunlight vitamin that most kids, tweens, and teens often lack from excessive indoor gadget time, nutritional voids, etc. As a result, Laliberte's (2010) "Problem Solved: Winter Blues from Prevention" insists that we must all ensure that our family members are digging it with vitamin D proactively since it is closely linked to keeping our serotonin levels elevated and balanced (p. 48). This connection is something super important in kids, tweens, and teens with ADHD for critical brain balance and overall wellness.

  Are you excited to dig it with D? Take a family hike, jog, stroll, or skate around the block. Find a local park and dive into the D!

- **Straight from the Hive:** Try warm milk with Manuka honey for a natural relaxer before bedtime with your kiddos. My girls really love it on bananas with peanut butter and chia seeds, too. You can also add it to evening herbal teas to evoke some sweet dreams and deeper sleep.

  As a slight disclaimer, because of honey's sugary contents, be sure to use a small amount, roughly the size of a poker chip. Just do not try to karaoke Lady Gaga's "Poker Face" song or you might lose face with older kids! BEE holistic, BEE well, and BEE wonderful when you try honey with your honey!

- **Sugar high:** As adults, we really need to embrace the "You are what you eat" mindset with all kids, especially those with ADHD. In turn, closely monitor sugar intake with their candies, sodas, caffeinated beverages, and all those ooey-gooey treats and desserts. Carefully monitor the number of fast foods you are serving your family, no matter how tempting or timesaving it may seem.

Studies encourage us to eat "clean," as clean as possible, rather than relying on fatty, greasy, and over-processed foods. Clean eating will naturally "eliminate unnecessary food additives such as artificial colors, flavors, sweeteners, and preservatives that do not add nutritional value and may contribute to ADHD symptoms. Limit sugar intake to 10% of total calories daily (roughly six teaspoons for children aged 2 to 19 years)" (Rucklidge, Taylor, and Johnstone, 2018, p. 16).

My daughters recently attended a birthday party with tons of sugary cakes, candies, and fruity drinks. They then began bitterly bickering in the car on the ride home to no avail from all the junk in the trunk (literally). Are you eager to crush that sugary rush and move toward mindful eating? I have been baking and cooking with dates as a natural sugar alternative when making muffins and other goodies lately. While I am not a professional cook or baker by any means, I encourage you to consult cookbooks at the local library freely or online that focus on mindful and natural ingredients to curb those high sugar sensations that tend to exacerbate ADHD! Be mindful when dining out, and always look for healthier family options.

Putting a freeze on fast food addictions can be so instrumental. La Valle's (1998) pioneering article from Drug Store News also indicates how high sugar intakes can cause low blood sugar and chromium depletion. The fast-food frenzy is really taking a toll on our kids as "The average American now consumes an average of 152.5 pounds of sugar in a year. That large soft drink at the drive-through window contains roughly 22 to 27 teaspoonfuls of sugar. It is reported that increased sugar intake increases urinary chromium excretion. Over time, this could have an impact on behavior" (CP13).

- **Move over:** Dairy overload can often cause major digestive issues. When kids are literally plugged up, they can act out even more. To counter these tummy troubles, consider some new dairy alternatives like almond, soy, coconut, cashew, and oat milk. I also suggest adding probiotics to your kiddos' diets with more kefir, Greek yogurt, and other mood foods. In my daughters' cases, they have been extremely helpful to tame tummies and boost moods. Let us Move over mindfully!

- **Veg heads:** You can opt for a Meatless Monday approach for more mindful family eating. Try to replace traditional noodles with veggies such as asparagus, zucchini, carrots, etc. Indulge in Brussels sprouts, cauliflower pizza crust, corns, asparagus, etc. Be a vicious veg head and also add more veggies to morning egg dishes, especially omelets. Make the Jolly Green Giant proud and be a veg head of household more often to facilitate holistic health and happiness in all kids, especially those with ADHD! My oldest daughter adores making and eating kale chips with me. She has recently been trying the freeze-dried snap peas too. We never know what they will like until we experiment, right? So, go beyond broccoli and green beans on your next grocery run!

In essence, it is highly advantageous to ensure that your kids, tweens, and teens are getting enough B vitamins in their diets:

a. B1 is closely linked to many key functions like immunity, heart support, and mental processing.

b. B2 offers energy, health for hair, skin, and eye.

c. B3 stabilizes our memories, moods, and hearts.

d. B5 can keep cholesterol levels in check.

e. B6 is an asleep reliever.

Are you ready for some "Sweet Dreams" by Queen B?

Finally, buzz with B-12 for increased mood and energy management. My young kids love the "classic ants on a log" snack with peanut butter, cashew butter, sunflower seed butter, or almond butter slathered onto celery with raisins, dried cherries, or cranberries. Have fun in the kitchen and make Rachael Ray proud healthily and mindfully today!

- **Beanie:** While I am not talking about the cool, fashionable hats, try to eat more mindfully against ADHD with beans and legumes. Make black beans burritos, hummus with chickpeas, serve up some edamame, and add lentils or sunflower seeds to beam up your families' diets!

- **Magnesium magnets:** Strive to add more magnesium into your family's overall dietary routines, especially in cases of ADHD. Studies describe how the average American is often highly deficient in magnesium "by about 70 mg daily. Magnesium is the calming mineral since it is the principal mineral used to control the parasympathetic nervous system. There is also the potential for calcium deficiency. Many children complain of aching legs and will see positive results with the initiation of a well-formulated multiple mineral supplement" (La Valle, 1998, CP13.). Get your magnesium magnets via food or supplements today!

- **Finding Nemo:** Set a habit to serve fatty fish to ramp up those Omegas and vitamin D 2–3 times a week. Yunus (2019) reminds us of compelling research that depicts how those with ADHD may have "lower levels of omega-3 fatty acids and higher levels of omega-6 that may lead to inflammation and oxidative stress."

  Accordingly, Evidence by Rucklidge, Taylor, and Johnstone (2018) also suggests that supplementation with omega-3s and/or a broad spectrum of micronutrients (for those not taking medication) may be beneficial for ADHD symptoms reduction. Still, it is so important that all "Patients should consult with their primary care provider before starting any supplement and with a dietician before changing their diet" (p. 15). Get your rod and reel in some fishing action during family meals and snacks for more mindful eating.

In fact, salmon nuggets and fish sticks are always major hits with my girls! They also enjoy coconut shrimp with fun and tasty dipping sauces. How can you get your Nemo and Dory on and blast more fish in your weekly menus?

- **See for yourself:** Fruits like pineapples, grapefruits, tomatoes, berries, mangoes, oranges, and kiwis, are a definite self-care saver for the blasts of vitamin C. I also recently discovered passion fruit, a rich source of beta-carotene and vitamin C, as recommended by the recent article aptly called "Mood Food" (2019) from Daily Mail.

- My girls love to toss some seeds onto their morning yogurt parfaits. Try some today and see for yourself if your kids will likely, say, "Yay!"

- **Zing with Zinc:** Assist your kids with ADHD in the culinary department to better zing against mood swings, common colds, flu, and other physical problems. Simply add more fruits and vegetables rich in zinc to their diets daily.

Honor the great pumpkin! Don't wait for Halloween and toss some pumpkin seeds to kids' sandwiches, baked goods, cereals, oatmeal, yogurts, pasta, salads, etc. Experts praise them for reducing feelings of anxiety (Mood Food, 2018), something that kids, tweens, and teens with ADHD know all too well, right? Let's zing and sing with zinc!

Chapter 17. Positive Environment and Emotional Development in Children

As a parent who intends to assist their child manages the symptoms associated with ADHD, one effective way to go about it would be to ensure the child's environment is well structured. Putting a wide range of environmental modifications in place would be of great help to the ward.

Environmental modifications mean that you would have to structure the child's environment to excel in other areas of their life. There are multiple settings where these strategies can take effect. That's why below are some tips that would help create a positive environment for a kid with ADHD.

Tips to Create a Positive Environment

- Structure and routine
- Breakdown of task
- Eliminate extra sounds
- Provide movement breaks
- Choose the right chores
- Repeat the process
- Strengthen the self-esteem of the child

Structure and Routine

Children with ADHD could use a structure and routine, which invariably helps them, especially as they find it challenging to stay organized.

The parent may need to organize the day for the child in order for the child to complete the assignment for the day. Also, during transitions, routines are of great importance. For instance, morning routines would help shape up the day for the child. Other routines that should not be ignored are the transition from home to school, bedtime routines, homework routines, and even TV routines. These routines would help the child get through the day and improve the general success of the day.

When it comes to school, there must be structure and routine as well. There might not also be options available to the child in their school.

Breakdown of Task

If there are assignments or large tasks at hand, a checklist is one way to break it down. It has been an effective way to remind the child of what they are expected to do at a particular point in time. Most of the time, checklists have been helpful or are more or less like a supportive tool for routines. For instance, a child might have a task list posted on the room door. Those task lists can be broken down into steps to enable the child to complete the overall task.

Most times, there's a misconception about children with ADHD. People feel they are incapable of attending to the right situations. However, it would interest you to know that ADHD in all verification makes it a bit tasking for them to do the right thing.

Eliminate Extra-Sounds

Children with ADHD find it difficult to assimilate what is happening in front of them, especially when there's outside noise. So, they might be having a lecture, and the teacher could be trying to give them instruction on how to approach an assignment or a lesson, but the child might be distracted. Thus, making it difficult to get the correct thing.

One way to help the child pull through these situations would be to eliminate those extra sounds that the child might be exposed to. Removing them or reducing them to the barest minimum would improve the child's chances of assimilating better with what is happening in the classroom.

Furthermore, when the child is trying to do their homework at home, one possible way to help the child would be to turn off the TV if it is switched on. Better still, the person hearing such a high volume should be handed an earpiece to ensure the environment remains quiet. If the child is trying to sleep, it is essential not to disturb them with unnecessary sounds, disrupting their sleep pattern.

Plus, it is advisable to keep the child away from the window or have it entirely closed to prevent any form of distraction from outside the premises or street. When it's time to do assignments or schoolwork at home, it is advisable to avoid having either an artwork or a brightly colored poster on the table as this could be a form of distraction to the child.

Provide Movement Breaks

Another way to help, especially during school or homework activities, is by providing movement breaks.

One of the usefulness of movement breaks for kids with ADHD is that it helps them focus more.

Movement breaks don't necessarily have to belong to a defined time limit as they can be five minutes, or at most ten minutes. Depending on where the child currently finds themselves, there is a different approach to this. For instance, if the child is at home, you can initiate physical activities like bike riding, walking, running, or playing basketball. However, during school hours, the child could take a quick stroll to get some water or, better still, go out to another marker for the teacher.

Choose the Right Chores

While other kids may have to do all kinds of chores, the case is different for kids with ADHD. Choosing appropriate assignments to aid their development in school or at home is advisable. Children with ADHD might struggle with sedentary tasks and perform well on active, hands-on chores. For example, the teacher might request them to either build a model or do a presentation. Doing so would succeed more than persuading the child to write on paper. While this sort of accommodation might not be available in all schools, it is still the parent's responsibility to request such a pattern for their children's class.

Repeat the Process

Creating a positive environment or putting a wide range of environmental modifications doesn't mean all the work is done. There's a tiny thing you might have to do, and that is to repeat the process. Sometimes, you might have done everything around the environment right, and thus, you would expect the child to be on the same page as you. However, it doesn't always work like that on kids with ADHD. They are usually prone to easily being distracted; thus, it is expected that you repeat the process, especially when it comes to directions.

Strength Self-Esteem

As a parent, it is important to strengthen the child's self-esteem. That's another part of building a positive environment for the child. Kids with ADHD usually end up at the receiving end of some negative feedback or criticism.

This is why you would have to spot opportunities where the child would have done something remarkable or correct, and thus, you must give specific feedback instantly without much delay. Detailed feedback is always a way to boost the child's self-esteem and encourage them to keep doing what you acknowledge is right. It could be "You did great with helping your uncle with his luggage" rather than saying "great job" without being specific.

You would agree that most individuals tend to fade everything into the background, especially when they put their mind on being focused on that particular time. However, this is not the case for individuals with ADHD. For them, everything around them stays foreground. It means that whatever noise they hear, whether far away or near, feels the same. So, you can have a concert in the next street going on, and their parents might be talking to them, both noises would appear to be the same. Helping your child by creating a positive environment cannot be over-emphasized.

How to Boost a Child's Self-Esteem

ADHD has long been associated with low self-esteem, emotional and physical issues. However, these problems are nothing to your child with ADHD until someone, including you, reminds them of their condition.

There is strength in everyone, whether you have ADHD or not. So, if your child feels incapable of their power to achieve or succeed, then chances are their condition worsens, and your relationship is threatened. Furthermore, it means the child loses interest and succumbs to whatever happens next.

As parents, it is disheartening when our child cannot move past the shackles of ADHD, but there is a simple solution. Employing positive language and attention are two ways to boost your child's self-esteem. The same impact is felt in a neurotypical child.

For children with ADHD, being available and in tune with your child's needs is a step to know how to boost their self-esteem and empower them. The truth is without this understanding of the emotional and physical turmoil; you will get overwhelmed soon and revert to aggressive parenting. Focusing on positive strengths points and minimizing weakness points is the way to boost self-esteem in children with or without ADHD. If we focus on problems, what we get is frustration; if we focus on opportunity, we get energy and positivity. Positive language and positive attention are skills to learn to empower our children to thrive and not survive.

The DRAFT Rule for Success

It is a simple acronym that attempts to empower the child with ADHD. The aim is to see their capabilities without comparing themselves to others regardless of their brain wiring.

D—Distinct

The missing link to our child's process is our attitude as parents. If we embrace them with positive vibes and energy, they absorb it and translate it into their lives. However, when we classify our kids as another ADHD case, we are oblivious of how we treat them or see how others treat them.

"D" stands for "Distinct," and your child with ADHD should know that they are unique, different from the crowd, and memorable. Yes, they should also know that their unique traits come with challenges, but it is within their power to control and make the best out of it.

One of the primary problems with ADHD is the focus, but it varies too. Some children with ADHD cannot focus on academic or school work but will do exceptionally well in sports. It is effortless. Their ability to zone in on one thing until they understand it could be the power. However, with schoolwork, their brains are everywhere. They are juggling several subjects even before they have the time to comprehend them fully. So, if your child does well in sports or hobbies, use that same tactic or strength to boost a weak area of their life.

R—Reasonable

How have you been unreasonable to your child's plight? A reasonable person is described as one that cautiously analyzes a situation and takes sensible steps to diffuse the problem. Many of us are blind to the plight of kids with ADHD and cannot understand, but we are not asking they should. We want parents to be reasonable and act as such. Remember, knowledge is power. Learning about ADHD will help us understand our children's behavior and be more reasonable in our judgment.

A—Assessable

Parents catering to ADHD children should help them access the best in life. Most people limit them by their vision of disorder or the symptoms. However, many children with ADHD are assessable for their quality, creativity, joy, approaches, and the good things of life.

F—Feasible

It means allowing your child to do what they can and gradually work up the ladder with every improvement. Most times, we want to push them into doing what they cannot or pursuing hobbies or quests that are physically, mentally, or emotionally incapable. It happens most of the time because we want them to be the image, we would like them to be and not like they are. Remember the "curious" secret key approach? Listen to them to discover who they are, what they want, and how they feel. Not what we want! Feasible tasks lead to boosting self-esteem in children. The contrary will lower self-esteem, making them a loser.

It can be viewed from two perspectives, and we will tackle each one. Parents should not push their kids who have ADHD into doing like the rest for fear of lack of time limitation, and they should not relax because of the condition either. Time limitation is a crucial factor when raising a child with ADHD, but we must endeavor to create a balance to have time for them to achieve a feat too.

The DRAFT is a step-by-step guide to enable parents to access their child's capability and put them on a cycle of success as they learn to overcome the challenges of ADHD.

Setting small goals and working up the difficulty levels enables them to learn to work to overcome obstacles.

This process breeds success.

Transforming Your Child's Apathy Into Engagement

Whether as toddlers, teenagers, or adults, apathy is of great concern raising a child with ADHD. Lack of care and motivation affects their academic, career, and daily activities. Most times, concerned parents use nagging, repeated lecturing, re-emphasizing, nudging, comparison, and a host of others. But it proves counterproductive and results in no results. However, when parents use the DRAFT rule, they give their kids control to manage their lives and take responsibility for their actions. All you have to do sometimes is take a step back and provide non-intrusive assistance while fulfilling your urge to be in charge.

How to Help Kids Feel Good About Themselves

- Help them learn no criticizing or nagging—TEACH.
- When teaching, SHOW, not just say, demonstrate, and then tell them to follow suit.
- Learn to commend them and do it wisely.
- Be the role model before anyone else.
- Stop harsh, crude, and rude criticism.
- Always look beyond the weakness and see strength in their action.
- Value their suggestions and accept their help.
- Give them space to reflect with your poke-nosing.

When parents understand Neuro-divergence, they relinquish the need to control every action their kids take. In our world, the brain of ADHD is like dotting parenting, and adding yourself to the equation does more harm than good. Please allow the child to make their own mistakes. It builds their confidence as they reflect on the whys and how to make it better.

It empowers them, builds their self-confidence, and imbibes responsibility in them. It helps the child learn, understand, and develop with your support. Whether neurotypical or neuro-diverse, kids will make mistakes. However, they will only learn in a loving environment where they are respected and acknowledged. As parents to AHDH children, developing their self-esteem and confidence starts young and begins with you.

Emotional Development in Childhood

You don't have to get a psychology degree to be a good parent, not even when you are parenting a child with ADHD (or any other disorder). However, learning more about how your child will develop will help you create the right environment for them. Remember that parenting a child with ADHD can be significantly different than parenting other children, so knowing about their emotional development becomes even more important.

As a result, we decided to devote an entire chapter to it: the emotional development of children in their first years of life (and why this is important for ADHD parenting).

Let's dig deeper and look at the skills and behaviors considered normal for kids in every age group.

From 0 to 12 Months

When kids are born, they are often referred to as "temperamental." They have very strong, contradictory emotions and don't know how to deal with their feelings.

They express negative emotions more easily than positive ones, which make them unpleasant to be around for anyone who doesn't want them as a friend. Because they have many of the same emotions as an adult, their expressions can be really confusing—for example, when they are fussy and crying and no one knows why.

Babies also have a self-soothing "mechanism," and they are at a phase where they are still learning a lot about the world (including how to differentiate facial expressions, for example). It is an age of marvel and discovery that borders on a miracle.

From 12 Months to 2 Years

From the time your child is one to two years old, you will start to notice that they can recognize their emotions more easily. They've also developed the ability to regulate them and keep their impulses in check.

They're capable of seeing things from other people's perspectives without completely losing touch with their own point of view. This is true empathy: recognition of another person's feelings based on your own perspective, without losing yourself entirely.

From 2 to 5 Years

The period from 2 to 5 is a time when children develop social skills. They will be able to read your moods and emotions and react accordingly.

They will start to develop self-control around the age of 4, but they will just have a "conscious" understanding of what this means and how it works.

Around the age of 5, kids also start to develop a conscience—it is at this point that they start feeling guilty after doing something wrong.

From 5 to 7 Years

The 5–7 years old period is one of the big changes in terms of emotional development.

Your child will start to read their parents' facial expressions and emotions better, and they will start to learn how to make friends. They will understand the world better and be more able to consider other people's points of view.

They will also develop a greater sense of control over their impulses, which can help them avoid acting impulsively.

From 7 to 10 Years

This is a period in which kids develop their capacity to show sympathy to others. They will also be better able to consider others' perspectives and understand how their actions affect other people.

From 10 to 13 Years

This is also a time of great changes in emotional development. Your child will be more able to identify their feelings and recognize other people's feelings. They will have a deeper understanding of how their actions affect other people.

They will also be able to manage their emotions better. Parents should make sure that they understand the meaning of words like anxiety, stress, and depression so they can express themselves and get help when needed.

From 13 Years Onwards

Your child will continue to develop into an adult, both emotionally and socially. They will have better emotional control and be able to make better decisions.

Though this period is often overlooked in families, it's a very important one for your child's development (and how they will behave as adults later on in life). Although at this point your child might be more independent, it is important to acknowledge that they might still need your help (even if they don't specifically ask for it). As a parent, you will have to find the fine balance between offering to help and allowing your child to learn how to stand on their own feet.

Keep in mind that these stages of emotional development are quite standard, but that doesn't mean that all children follow the same patterns. In the case of a child with ADHD, it is important to help them build on what's normal for them. They may never be able to be as social as other children, but you can help them find balance and be as efficient as possible at acquiring friends and building steady relationships, for example.

You cannot expect things to happen to the textbook in the case of a child with ADHD. But you can expect them to eventually develop healthy emotions and ways of coping with their emotions from multiple points of view.

Chapter 18. Inner Space and Being

Perhaps you are beginning to see the impact your inner life has on your outer life. To make sense of our world and all activities are available to our consciousness, the brain creates perspectives, artificial constructions that provide a fixed point, and the idea of a separate self from which to send and receive perceptions.

Speaking for myself, I am usually aware of the great world of possibilities, and therefore I do not feel limited by this idea. On the contrary, pure consciousness is still available when I recognize this. Still, when I'm preoccupied or absorbed in the details of perspective, it narrows into my figurative field of vision, and I start to feel squeezed or trapped.

Our human creative property is embedded in the very nature of consciousness. As a result, properties of the individual perspective that we occupy support and nurture the creation of those properties in our experience. This happens through small fundamental processes that are generally beyond the reach of our practical consciousness, but that come to define and describe our experience, also known as our interpretation of life itself. This dynamic is only one part of a complex dynamic referred to in the ancient Hermetic teaching, "As inside, so outside."

When ADHD symptoms are present and unwanted, it is clear that you, or the person suffering from it, may be limited by the thinking brain, effectively limiting a new stream of pure awareness. A person with ADHD may experience these states as if they are magnified. Potentially, an even more dramatic shift occurs when you move from thought-bound awareness—or what is a wing of awareness—to influence or even dissolve the perspective we once created.

Giving awareness to the formation of our perspectives, whether in hindsight or as we observe them, determines the clarity of consciousness available to our perception at any moment.

One trick is to advance the lighter emotions, which are less dense than the heavier emotions we associate with negativity. That is a simple way to start. By itself, feeling good can be a helpful benchmark for work.

For example, suppose I am standing in a rushing river where I have never been before. In that case, the currents can seem threatening, and the slippery rocks are like insidious enemies leading me into danger. This feels sinister, and perhaps upon reading that, her body tensed, and her awareness intensified. But, on the other hand, I can choose to see the current situation a little differently.

If I'm in the same case but not resisting the present—rather than following it and fully engaging it without making my situation dangerous—slippery rocks feel silly and fun. I can go in and out of currents and depths without feeling threatened. I may find myself surrendering to some—allowing them to help me on my way.

You can say that how you feel about the form of reality around you helps determine your perspective and experience. It is the container where it happens.

Anyone who perceives profound and practical teaching from the words above might also perceive the education that ADD, or its presence in others, offers toward our human experience. Let me explain. As a metaphor, attention can be likened to an aperture through which our life experience unfolds, except that this is no ordinary lens one merely peers through. Instead, attention draws both perceiver and the perceived into one creative field balanced, as the beheld and beholder.

Within this field, this container, if you will, there emerges what each perceiving being considers to be their life. From this perspective, we can glimpse both our divine power and our mortal limitation, the entire spectrum of our existence, indeed. Viewed power, free will presents us with the ability to create our own experience by creating and choosing our perceptions.

In limitation, free will offers only our choices to act within a fixed perception. However, it was served and is simply accepted to be. In the first, you co-create by being consciously aware of creative opportunities. In the latter, you create only interpretations based on thoughts: judgments, reactions, and past perceptions.

Presently, Western medicine understands ADHD as a syndrome, a group of symptoms that occur together and for which there is no single known cause or cure. As one that struggles with ADD, I can say with compassion and humility that I'm grateful there's no known cure since, to me, ADHD can only be known as a state of being... And I, for one, might take exception to there being a cure for that!

To blend some science and experience, I offer these few observations. Currently, ADD is recognized by distractibility, impulsivity, and a myriad of other related expressions. You can say that these symptoms arise as they contrast with, or challenge, the accepted boundaries of a perspective that formed to contain what is deemed necessary or appropriate.

One insight or tip I suggest is to balance one's perception; a person must intentionally offer equal measures of open-hearted awareness. Failing to do so by intention will keep us out of balance and locked in a narrower perspective. This narrowness itself results in some inevitable clashes with the spacious contents of the perceived world.

If such a "standard" brain function existed, even my perception of being in dangerous waters where mere objects were staged as enemies could be tempered by other parts of my brain involving and processing a somewhat less black and white situation.

For many with ADHD, the neurochemicals that engage those supporting parts of the brain shut off, and the same transmitters intensify a smaller area of their brain activity. When this happens within an individual, perhaps he is aware that other options for perception may exist. Still, they are not apparent through the brain activity that is offered at the moment. The result is this magnifying effect—a fact that I use as a metaphor to describe some aspects of the ADD experience. This can precede the authentic perceptions of being stuck in a cycle of negative thought that is interpreted as being caused or created by negative manifestations.

Someone experiencing ADHD symptoms can learn to begin to recognize them as a type of warning. Response or phenomenon, which informs them they are stuck in thinking. When this occurs, they could use some physical change to invite space, in other words, fresh awareness, to unlock the brain's grip on one set of perceptions.

This is a self-awareness practice that is recommended for anyone and is especially helpful in relationships for someone else to use on themselves first, for example, when ADHD symptoms are visible in their spouse. This is a metaphor comparable to the instruction you would see when donning your oxygen mask first in the event of an onboard emergency, such as securing your own oxygen mask before proceeding to help others.

This focus on yourself first allows you to be more present and less vulnerable to an unwanted negative exchange. In turn, your self-leadership models for your spouse (and everyone else) a way of being that is better known by experience than by description or direction. Like inside, it's outside.

The application of modeling in relationships can seem subtle but can have a profound and lasting impact on you, your partner, and your relationship. It changes any dynamic where the perception of right and wrong, good or bad, or roles in a pecking order are hard to break out of.

All of these can create resentments and misunderstandings from both sides, and where these areas manifest problems; they are usually indicators of egos requiring something to be a certain way. Modeling is a genuine expression, and as intended, free of manipulation or expectation of any specific result. Unfortunately, the ego does not understand modeling. Its best attempt to emulate it will look like trying to control an outcome rather than empowering the authentic creation of lasting change.

Our human ego creeps in by adjusting only behavior that is already anticipating a specific result. Doing this reflects an already diminished view of possibility and, as such, presents new limitations. Even though our experience may support the small-sights idea as we advance, ultimately, it disempowers all that surrounds it, not just the object of its gaze. The compulsion or the need to already know how something will receive something or the outcome will ensure that result.

At the core of this desire for control is resistance to allow what wants to happen, obscuring the flow of awareness when the ego is triggered to defend some long-held belief.

These dynamics can be especially apparent in family relationships or long-standing established marital or partnered relationships. These become an issue, particularly when imbalanced, as gains are perceived in other areas of your life, yet we appear or feel trapped when these older and deeper relationships engage.

Often, an opening that allows for the breakdown of just one of those resistance points in a previous relationship, say one with a parent, will recognize in such stark contrast to last thought patterns that it will be considered a remarkable advance. It weakens reason over other past resistance points, and the relationship is seen as transformed.

Decades of study of persuasion or control teach us simply let go, allowing everyone to be what they really are. When you let go or effectively limit another person, the beliefs and expectations you place on him can begin to fall away.

Like so many other facets and dynamics, this is true in all relationships, especially concerning a person with ADHD. When even the subtlest perception of resistance or conflict arises for someone, whose primary challenge exists in regulating attention can lose the opportunity for change. This truth is expressed in the adage; energy flows where attention goes and is also borne out in reverse—attention flows where energy goes.

Once triggered, no matter how reasonable other perspectives may be, at the moment, the person with ADD has difficulty perceiving the interaction as anything other than a conflict. Once that judgment forms, it must dissipate, often slowly, as circumstances and events allow a free flow of awareness to enter perception, eventually.

This repair of perception is a way of enabling natural healing that some doctors refers to when autonomous resources alone are sufficient to rebalance and restore the health of the body. It will work on its own if we simply give it the time and space to do it. In the brain or in the psychic part of the body.

Conflict and resistance are manifested through resistant thoughts and behaviors into the brain and the psychic part of the body. In turn, it can eventually be carried to other parts of the body to manifest as illness or disease from within.

Managing Morale

Morale is associated with energy, mood, drive, agency, motivation, timing, and quality of life. In the military, morale is related to the will to fight. For us, morale is associated with the choice to keep working around obstacles until we reach our goals. For people already facing an uphill struggle with ADHD, morals can be the deciding resilience factor.

Morale is associated with will, desire, meaning, confidence, and motivation.

When morale is up, we are more likely to believe in our ability to realize our goals. Conversely, when morale is low, we might feel like giving up rather than persisting.

Morale is related to how we take care of ourselves as well as how we motivate ourselves. People with ADHD can be particularly vulnerable to demoralization. If you have ADHD, you must monitor and protect your morale. When you advocate for and are kind to yourself, you are protecting your morale.

Motivational states are like battery packs supplying the energy we need to move forward toward a goal-directed future. Motivational states provide the power to overcome obstacles and delay gratification. Unfortunately, people with ADHD have an impaired ability to picture the intended future while simultaneously engaging with boring details in the present. The inability to sustain motivation can drain your batteries and lower your morale.

You will discover some workarounds for the following morale related obstacles:

- You don't use to pay attention to your morale
- You are still troubled by memories of being discouraged in the past
- Chronic stress is bad for your morale
- Keeping your energy up can be difficult when there are many (often dull) steps on the path toward a goal
- You have difficulties staying motivated

You feel beaten down and demoralized by ADHD.

ADHD cannot demoralize you. If you feel frustrated, it is probably due to something you have control over. Below are some possible sources of demoralization to be curious about.

- How you take care of yourself
- How you motivate yourself
- How forgiving you are of yourself
- How you show up as your own friend
- Who do you listen to?

You don't have to pay attention to your morale.

Here is an exercise to help you monitor your morale.

Directions: Set your intention to notice how you take care of yourself. The questions below can serve as a guide.

- How do you tend to treat yourself when you make mistakes?
- Would you be comfortable treating someone else this way?

- How do you tend to treat yourself when you succeed? E.g., do you give yourself credit where credit is due?
- Do you give yourself as much credit as you make criticism? (What is the ratio)?

How Do You Tend to Treat Yourself When You Make Mistakes?

You are haunted by memories of being demoralized in the past. Send your past self some empathy.

Now that you know something about ADHD, you can better sense the challenges you faced earlier in your life. This exercise offers you a chance to send your past self some warmth and empathy. You can even boost your morale in a memory. Try this exercise below only if you are comfortable exploring these memories. If you feel you are not ready, please stop.

Think of any ADHD-related incidents that happened when you were young in such a way that, when you remember it, you still feel a little bad about it. Perhaps you felt like giving up after dropping the ball on something, or you were scattered at a time when it was important to be focused. Maybe you were embarrassed about forgetting something important. Someone may have made fun of you for being spacey.

Did you assume that you were irresponsible or lazy, etc.?

Picture your past self in that scene.

Imagine speaking warmly to your past self (privately or out loud).

Start sentences with the phrase, "No wonder..."

E.g. "No wonder it is so hard for you to sit still in school. You have ADHD," or, "No wonder you are so overwhelmed. You try so hard, yet you end up late because you don't know that you have ADHD." The empathy is in the "No wonder you..."

Now picture how your past self-responds to warmth and empathy. This memory has been altered.

You get stingy when it comes to giving yourself credit.

Do you tend to discount the importance of small steps that you make? (E.g. you withhold giving yourself credit until you have completed your goal.)

Workaround.

Acknowledge any effort that you make, no matter how small.

Since tiny accomplishments can still involve high degrees of difficulty (especially for the organizationally impaired), you give yourself credit (where credit is due). This is a resilience factor that is within your control.

Try the experiment below to experience how savoring credit can affect you:

1. Write down any three things that you expended any energy on today, no matter how small.
2. Look at them one at a time.
3. Take a few breaths as you savor each one.
4. Notice how it feels to allow yourself to savor your efforts.
5. At the end of the day, write everything you expended any energy on all day (no matter how small). Include anything you might tend to take for granted, like parenting, chores, or going to work. Even contemplating something counts.

6. As you savor this list, notice whether the energy level in your body matches the efforts you expended and acknowledged.

7. Keeping your energy up can be difficult when there are many (often boring) steps on the path toward a goal.

8. Have fun! Protect your morale by making sure you are having fun whenever possible. Spice up the path with what makes you smile. Listen to music. Make up a game. Fun is an essential strategy for sustaining attention.

9. You have difficulties with self-motivation.

We can better maintain higher levels of motivation at the beginning (idea) stage of a project. However, we can quickly lose that motivation during the later stages.

Motivational styles matter when considering their impact over time.

Negative motivation (stress, harshness, fear), for example, may be effective motivators in the short term but harmful in the long term. It is helpful to monitor your motivational style. Once you can monitor it, you can fine-tune it.

Notice how you tend to motivate yourself.

Directions: Try to pay attention to how you motivate yourself (using the question provided below). The goal is to observe, not change. It might be helpful to write the question down and stick it in your pocket as a reminder.

It would be ideal for keeping a log.

- Do you motivate yourself with stress?
- Do you encourage yourself?
- Do you acknowledge your progress to yourself?

- Do you tend to play to win or not to lose?
- Do you tend to motivate yourself positively or negatively?
- Do you tend to push or pull yourself toward goals?

Protect your morale by taking charge of keeping yourself motivated. You can do this by building motivation into organization systems, externalizing big picture goals, and making fun of action plans, for example.

I have come across many people with ADHD caught in a cycle of trying and failing. I remember someone telling me, "You can only hit your head against the wall so many times before you give up." This is what it means to be frustrated. The problem is that the majority of these people assumed that they were discouraged because they had ADHD.

Demoralization is not a symptom of ADHD! It is more likely the result of doing what doesn't work over and over again. Ultimately, your morale will suffer if you are expecting yourself to get over your ADHD and function like an average person. You will enhance your morale each time you work around your ADHD.

Pathways to Action

Pathways to action are how you get to your goal. These means involve methods, strategies, and systems of organization. "To do" are pathways to action. Even If your goal is to enjoy a relaxing vacation in Hawaii, you will still have to manage lots of details before you can unpack your flip-flops.

People with ADHD need specialized pathways. It is possible that they do not achieve their goals because they are trying to follow the same paths that ordinary people use without modifying them to be compatible with themselves.

- Pathways can become slippery slopes.

- A common error made by people with ADHD is to take on too much at once.
- You can set yourself up for failure by following ADHD-unfriendly pathways to action.
- Your brain is organizationally challenged.
- To-do lists can be handy. They can also become oppressive and de-motivational.
- Your mind is susceptible to being organized by the external environment.

Pathways to action can turn into slippery slopes.

It is risky to follow a pathway to action without determining whether or not it is ADHD-friendly. Ways to action are fraught with challenges for people with ADHD. We are at risk of becoming mired in the details involved with the path such that we lose track of the destination.

Make sure that pathways to action are ADHD-friendly or can be modified to become ADHD-friendly. A common error made by people with ADHD is to take on too much at once.

Try to bite off less than you can chew. See if you can do less than you think you are capable of. This may be harder than you think. You are more likely to fail when following pathways designed for ordinary people. By relying on ADHD-unfriendly pathways, you may be setting yourself up for failure.

For example, normal people can innately estimate the amount of time it will take to get ready for something. People with ADHD who rely on their innate ability to know how much time it will take to prepare for something will probably be late and/or unprepared.

Chapter 19. No-Drama Disciplines

Make the Instructions Clear

Often, the instructions some parents give their kids might not be clearly understood based on how they were given. Therefore, for kids with ADHD, one of the best ways of disciplining them is by providing laid-out instructions. This set of rules will be unambiguous and concise so that the kids can easily remember. Just a few but clear and simple rules are the best way for a Neuro-divergent brain to assimilate. Set the rules with your child and not against him. If you involve him in the process of setting rules is the best you can do for him and you.

Comment Your Child's Effort

Kids with ADHD struggle with different things daily. You must show them all the support they need without making them feel weird. If there is a time when the kid handles a situation correctly, you should commend their efforts. Your reward can even go as far as getting one of the things they have always longed for. Remember to express your approval using the specific sentence, do not say "Wow, well done" but instead use more specific like: "Wow, I'm glad you were able to solve (indicate specific situation/problem) on your own, and with the right attitude, that's great." By doing so, you make him feel that you care about his behavior.

Overlook Some Mild Behaviors

We were all kids once; now, imagine if your parents hammered every little mistake you made. It can be overwhelming living in such a house. In the same vein, some mild behaviors of your child can also be overlooked. However, you need to draw the line when those behaviors become constant and more glaring.

Break Complex Tasks Into Simple Ones

Since one of the issues with children with ADHD is attention, you need to sustain their interest by breaking their responsibilities into easy-to-understand tasks. This way, they can follow through with their chores and other duties without getting confused. It's a fundamental strategy to break a task into a small, specific task. It is something to apply forever for an ADHD person; it enables them to accomplish the task.

Organize Their Lives

Having a kid with ADHD means that you put in twice the effort to help them stay structured and aligned with them. Helping them sort out their day is one way of ensuring you discipline them. As you instruct them and plan their days, it begins to stick with them, and it gets to a point where they can plan their days themselves. Therefore, the constant display of the kids in the right way will ensure they find coping mechanisms to evade the excesses of ADHD

Talk With Your Child

Communicating effectively with your child is a great way to discipline them also. Knowing how to communicate with them can position you to become a better parent and understand the child's reasoning. It can help uncover different mysteries that you thought could not be solved. We wrote chapters on Positive Language and Positive Attention, how to talk to children, and the 3-Secret Keys to help you communicate with your beloved, unique child. For the right balance, we will also look at some of the things you should not do in the guise of disciplining your kid.

Discipline Don't

Don't Show Your Frustration

Remember, we talked about having patience when dealing with children who have ADHD. You need to keep calm and refrain from lashing out. There will be instances where the information you have shared is not understood or misinterpreted. You do not need to be angry or lash out. Simply explain in more straightforward terms to the kid so they can get the task done.

Avoid Negative Words

It can be stressful trying to organize your life as a parent and doing the same for your child. It takes even more sacrifice to manage the child with ADHD. As a result of the clutter and other discomforts that you may feel, avoid using negative words on and around them.

They already feel judged for the disorder, and the one place they think they can find solace should not make them feel like an outsider. Parents can quickly lose children with negative words, especially where the child finds it difficult to curtail the excesses of their disorder.

You Don't Need to Yell

It might sound absurd for some parents but dealing with an ADHD kid means you have to refrain from some parenting style. You can't afford to yell as this pushes them away.

As much as their disorder is on the inside, treating the kids without labeling them ensures a better life for them.

Forget About the Small Things

There is no need to yell at a child with ADHD to complete two out of three given tasks. You can forget the one they did not do. Asides from chores, parents should understand that there may be times when kids with ADHD may forget the small stuff, and you need to move past them. Although subtly bringing their notice to these things will train their minds, in general, if it can be overlooked, please do so.

Applying these tips should be easier to discipline without drama and get the best out of our child.

Conclusion

ADHD is a very common diagnosis that has many long-term effects. It affects where a person's attention span and impulse control are located. It can impact relationships with others, school performance, and even the medical care they receive in the future. ADHD is not like any other illness because of these types of symptoms that it brings about for those who have it.

There are numerous approaches to living with ADHD as an adult. There are various medications that you can take as well as other options such as lifestyle changes, therapy, or going to support groups for people who may be struggling with ADHD themselves. Another option is to not raise children who have ADHD because it can be very hard for the parents and the child both since they will have to try very hard to correct the problem.

If raising a child with ADHD is expected, it is important to make sure they are educated on how ADHD works and how they can overcome it. Being aware of their problems and making them aware of their strengths will help raise an adult that will be successful while having these symptoms. Parents need to provide their children with enough support that they do not feel alone when they struggle with what they are going through. Children with ADHD will be fine as long as they know this information early on in life so that they can work around the issues brought by them.

As a parent of a child with ADHD, there are many different ways how to help your child become successful. It is not up to one or two different ways, but it may take some time to find out what works for your child. You should be ready for anything when it comes to having a child with ADHD because their symptoms can change quickly and all of the sudden. When raising them it is very important to keep them engaged in activities and encourage them in what they do so that they are happy and can stay positive about themselves along the way.

As a parent of a child with ADHD, it is important to realize that some of their symptoms may come full circle and may be hard to watch if they choose to act out. Accepting that this is happening and that they are unable to express their feelings or behaviors with others might be challenging for them. As a parent, you need to support them in ways such as encouraging them about their outcomes in school, what goals they have for themselves or others and giving them simple facts and information on how ADHD affects you and your family's life.

Sometimes the best way to raise them is the same way they were raised by another person instead of trying to change how they were raised. Sometimes it may only be a matter of time before the symptoms come full circle and cause them to act out all over again. If this is something you want to prevent from happening, anger management skills are very important for a parent, especially in how they direct their anger toward their children.

Made in the USA
Monee, IL
27 November 2022